W9-CPV-600

Living CLEAN

THE JOURNEY CONTINUES

World Service Office
PO Box 9999
Van Nuys, CA 91409
TEL (818) 773-9999
FAX (818) 700-0700
WEB www.na.org

World Service Office–Canada
Mississauga, Ontario

World Service Office–Europe
Brussels, Belgium
TEL +32/2/646-6012

World Service Office–Iran
Tehran, Iran
WEB www.na-iran.org

Printed in China.
24 23 22 21 18 17 16 15

ISBN 978-1-55776-927-5 (Hardcover) WSO Catalog Item No. 1150
ISBN 978-1-55776-928-2 (Softcover) WSO Catalog Item No. 1151
ISBN 978-1-55776-965-7 (ePub) WSO Catalog Item No. 1152

This is NA Fellowship-approved literature.

Table of Contents

Preface xi

Chapter One

Living Clean ... 1

NA *offers us a path, a process, and a way of life. The work and rewards of recovery are never-ending. We continue to grow and learn no matter where we are on the journey, and more is revealed to us as we go forward. Finding the spark that makes our recovery an ongoing, rewarding, and exciting journey requires active change in our ideas and attitudes. For many of us, this is a shift from desperation to passion.*

Keys to Freedom 4

Growing Pains 8

A Vision of Hope 13

Desperation to Passion 16

Why We Stay 19

Chapter Two

The Ties That Bind ... 23

In recovery, we are free to explore and to consider who we are and who we want to become. The changes we experience in the process can feel pretty disruptive to our identity and our relationships, but through that struggle we find that our acceptance, love, and faith continue to grow. Though our goals and our methods may vary, what we have in

common are the tools and principles that allow us to be who we are. Together we rise to a point of freedom.

Connection to Ourselves 24
Connection to a Higher Power 28
Connection to the World Around Us 33
Connection to Others 37

Chapter Three
A Spiritual Path.......................................45

The spirituality we experience in NA is simple and practical: It allows us to live in harmony with our world and to experience empathy and compassion for others. The steps are a path to spiritual growth; we awaken to our own spirituality. As we develop a relationship with a Higher Power in whatever way we understand that, we come to understand that our spirituality is not a part of our lives; it is a way of life that brings us to an understanding of our purpose and the freedom we had been seeking all along.

Awakening to Our Spirituality 46
A Spiritual, Not Religious Program 49
A Spiritual Journey 54
Spirituality Is Practical 59
Walking the Walk 62
Spirituality in Action 67
Conscious Contact 73
Creative Action of the Spirit 76

Chapter Four
Our Physical Selves 83

Learning to live in our bodies isn't easy. We haven't been kind to them, and often they bear the painful scars of our addiction. Making

peace with our physical selves is necessary for our physical survival—but it is also a part of our amends process, an act of self-acceptance, and a way we experience freedom, healing, and joy. This chapter addresses the way we treat ourselves in recovery, learning to find pleasure in being physically alive and aware—and facing our aging, our vulnerability, and our mortality.

It's a Relationship 85
Letting Ourselves Go 87
Sex 91
Thrill-Seeking and Adventure 95
Wellness and Health 97
Illness 101
Disability 106
Emotional and Spiritual Crisis 110
Aging 113
Death, Dying, and Living with Grief 115
Courage 120

Chapter Five
Relationships.................................... 123

Our recovery is based in relationships, and most of us struggle with them in one way or another. Our relationships with one another in the rooms, with the families we come from and the families we create, are all places where we learn to practice principles, including honesty, empathy, and intimacy. Love is a healing presence in our lives, and we experience its power when we allow ourselves to reach out.

Fellowship 126
Friendship 132
Bridging Two Worlds: Relationships Outside NA 139
Family 141

As we get some time in recovery, we get some time in the world as well. Social acceptability does not equal recovery, to be sure, but that doesn't mean they're mutually exclusive, either: For many of us it is something we must learn along the way. Our work habits and our beliefs about work, education, money, and stability change and grow as we stick around—sometimes in surprising ways. Learning to deal with success and failure, with risk and responsibility, with stability and change are all part of the process some of us call "growing up in recovery."

Chapter Seven

The Journey Continues............................ 219

From the first time we find hope, we are in an ongoing process of spiritual awakening that can last our whole lives, if we are willing. Continuing to feel that our recovery is alive requires us to keep growing. Isolation and complacency hold us back from freedom in ways we may not even feel until we are stuck. Generosity of spirit is the antidote for loneliness and alienation. Being of service frees us into our own lives and opens us to the spirit of love that surrounds us. We experience unconditional hope and understand that there is no limit to how much better we can get. No matter how far we have come, the journey continues.

Awakenings 219
Living Our Principles 222
The Lifelong Practice of Surrender 227
Complacency 229
Setting Ourselves Apart 232
Keeping It Real 237
Being of Service 242
Principles, Practice, and Perspective 248
Love 254

Preface

Our Basic Text assures us that more will be revealed, and our experience bears that out. More has been revealed in the years since those words were written, and more continues to be revealed every day that we live clean and practice the principles of recovery. We grow as individuals, and we also grow and mature as a fellowship. As we learn from our experience, we pass on that knowledge. This means that each generation of newcomers has more resources available in NA than the one before. Whether this strengthens or weakens us depends entirely on how well we understand our primary purpose and practice the principles of sharing, caring, and service.

Our greatest treasure and resource is the depth of our personal knowledge of the recovery process. We share that treasure at meetings, at our celebrations, over coffee, and in our literature. Once again, we offer in written form as much as we can of our collective experience, strength, and hope. This book, written by addicts for addicts, is a snapshot of our fellowship: addicts in recovery who have helped each other face life on its own terms, without the use of drugs, for consecutive days, months, years, and decades. It is intended both as an offering to new members and to rekindle the passion of our oldtimers. It could not possibly contain all that our members know or believe, but it does reflect what we have been discovering and sharing since 1982, when our Basic Text was approved.

The first draft of a book titled "Living Clean" was created in 1983, but the history of this project goes back even further. As our Basic Text, *Narcotics Anonymous*, was being written, some of our members knew that it would not be our last word on the subject of living the NA way. The versions that were created in 1983 and 1990 contained a lot of concrete advice, suggestions, and rules for how to get clean and stay clean. But most of us don't follow rules very well. Our experience is sometimes very different from what we wish were true about the process. We found that what we share in common are not the particular actions we take, but the principles we try to practice as we live. In the years that have followed, generations of addicts have gotten clean and stayed clean using the Basic Text as our guide, and that experience has given us a perspective on the principles of recovery unlike any other.

We knew from the beginning that we were describing a problem not related to any single substance, but a disease that, left untreated, would manifest in one symptom or another until it killed us. A focus on one symptom or substance is too narrow for us. Just as we understand that addiction affects all aspects of our lives, we can see that recovery affects everything we do. Our relationships with our families, our work, our spirituality—even our own bodies—are profoundly shaped by where we come from and the ways in which we address our disease. Just as the rewards of our recovery are often beyond our wildest dreams, we know that the impact of our recovery on our own lives and on those around us is beyond measure. We may never know the good we do just by staying clean and living a principled life to the best of our ability. Our gratitude for our new way of life motivates us to keep giving more, living more, and loving more.

We are called to tell our story in NA not just once, but over and over. We cannot see the entirety of ourselves in one Fifth Step or one share, and we can't see the entirety of our recovery all at once, either. We see it in layers, and our vision of ourselves changes each time we have a shift in perspective or a change in perception. Telling the truth about our lives is one of the most powerful things we can ever do. We start to see the threads that run through our experience, even though we may feel like we have been many different people over the course of our lives. We can see the patterns that help us or hold us back, and we can find hope even at times when our lives are very difficult.

Recovery is a full-contact, lifelong process. The more serious we are about it, the more clearly we can see how much growth is still available to us, no matter where we are on the journey. We are never done learning. Continued practice of the program of Narcotics Anonymous doesn't just make our lives easier. It makes them richer, better, and more interesting. We begin by staying clean, and from there the program gives us the tools we need to find the answers that are right for us. Different moments teach us, reach us, or help us break through. We hope that the experience we share here will serve to propel our members forward, beyond what we know now.

This book is not a catalog of advice, but rather a collection of experience, strength, and hope about living clean as we experience it in our daily lives, in our relationships, and in our service to others. Not everything in the pages that follow will be equally important to everyone. Each of us has different challenges on our journey. However, we hope that there is something here for every member.

What follows is the experience of many addicts from all over the world. Hundreds of members shared their insight on living clean in workshops, letters, conversations, electronic bulletin boards, and audio recordings. The book took shape as it developed. As our journey continued, the focus of *Living Clean* shifted as well. The content and structure changed according to the input. The process swung the doors open, and we were amazed at what developed. We learned from one another, and the sum was greater than its parts. The common thread through our varied experience is that we continue to draw strength from NA no matter how much cleantime we have, no matter how many steps we have worked, and no matter where life takes us. Sharing our experience gives it meaning and value. And the deep relationships we form in NA—with one another, with ourselves, and with our Higher Power—become more valuable than we can imagine. We stay connected with the program and the fellowship over many years because we find what we need here. Where once we may have wondered how we could ever make NA a part of our lives, now many of us cannot imagine our lives without it. When we use the tools available to us, our recovery continues to thrive no matter what we face or how long we stay clean.

The most important thing about living clean is that we are alive to do it, and for people with the disease of addiction this is nothing less than a miracle. We do recover to live full and rewarding lives. Those lives present us with challenges, some of which we never expected. Living beyond our wildest dreams often means that we are in uncharted territory. The countless addicts who have contributed to this book have made clear that the miracle of getting clean is not the last one we experience, or the last one we need. We have learned that we really can survive anything and stay clean. It's never too late to start over, reconnect with the fellowship, work steps, have a spiritual awakening, and find a new way to live. As long as we are willing to stay clean and keep coming back, our recovery continues to unfold in ways we couldn't imagine. We are living clean, and every day the journey continues.

Living Clean

Living clean is a lifelong journey, and the NA program gives us tools to build a life infused with hope. No matter where we are on our journey, we believe that it can get better, and that we can get better. We practice living a principled life and find a new way to live. We try new things, and some of them suit us better than others. As we experience living clean with its ups and downs, miracles and struggles, dead ends and open doors, we see the world more clearly and better understand our place in it.

The program of Narcotics Anonymous is the way we have found to escape lives of desperation and pain. But that's not all NA is: It's a path, a process, and a way of life. Many of us come in with just the barest hope that we can get the pain to stop. In the beginning, our willingness is born of our suffering and fear. Living the program changes us in ways we might expect, and in ways we never imagined.

NA gives us the ability to turn our desperation into a passion to live fully and grow spiritually. We experience relief almost from the beginning of our recovery, and our first experiences of joy are like seeing color for the first time. Our minds are open and our spirits are free. Even if we experience it only for fleeting moments, that joy carries us through our hardest days and nights.

It's not what we think about our recovery that matters; it's what we do. Living clean is a spiritual process, and it teaches us that the world is bigger than we imagined and not as far out of reach as we had feared. Our flawed beliefs about people who didn't use drugs shaped our opinions about what we might be like when we stopped. When we first got clean, many of us worried that our lives were about to become small and boring. What we find really is beyond our wildest dreams. We have opportunities and the ability to follow through on them. Perhaps more importantly, our connections with people become intensely important and satisfying to us. The close friendships we have with members who share our recovery can be a deeper connection than family. We share an intimacy that is really special, and when we carry that over the course of many years, it grows into an abiding affection and understanding of one another.

Commitment to recovery is essential for us. Maintaining recovery as a priority may come to mean different things for us over time. We need to maintain our connection to NA, but taking responsibility for our lives also matters. So many things compete for our attention, and as addicts we have a tendency to think in extremes: all or nothing, right or wrong. Finding the balance is an ongoing negotiation.

Attending meetings regularly doesn't have to mean every night of the week, but meetings continue to matter for our own well-being and for our ability to carry the message. Keeping that lifeline strong and ready is a matter of continuing maintenance. It gets easier when we let go of the idea that it ought to be hard. After many years of recovery, a member shared that he was finally able to answer the question "Is it possible that life is really this simple?" with a simple "Yes."

The principles we practice in NA have meaning throughout our lives. They offer us a way to stop using and to free ourselves to be ourselves. Working the steps, studying the traditions, and applying ourselves to service in and out of NA helps us to discover who we are and what we believe. Carrying the message brings us awareness of our gifts and limitations, and guides us to change.

We can measure our lives not in years or by the things we gain or lose, but by the degree to which we make peace with our own lives and the world around us. Spiritual growth is the real success. As our recovery unfolds, we find ourselves resolving feelings we never admitted we had. Open-mindedness gives us the ability to see more and more clearly within ourselves as we go through the never-ending process of surrendering, taking inventory, and inviting change.

The message we carry has three parts: Any addict can stop using, lose the desire to use, and find a new way to live. We talk a lot about the first two, because stopping is an emergency when we get here, and losing the obsession is necessary for us to enjoy our lives. But the hard work does not end there. Finding a new way to live is not something we do just once. Some of us experience great upheaval as we try again and again to find a life that makes sense for us. But we continue to carry the message, using our experience to help others. The more experience we have to share, the richer our message can become.

Keys to Freedom

As we practice these principles in all our affairs, they gain traction in our lives, and they start feeling more natural. For example, in the beginning we may have to consciously practice being honest. As we continue this practice, we find dishonesty progressively more uncomfortable, perhaps even agonizing; and gradually we notice that honesty has become more normal for us. We are basically honest people, and we even like it. Some say this is how we know a Higher Power is involved. When our defects are removed, we may not feel them go. We may not even notice the change unless we fall back into old behavior and find that it is no longer comfortable or workable for us. We call our sponsor in distress over having "done it again," or even because we are thinking about acting on that old defect, and realize how long it has been since that behavior had crossed our minds. Learning to survive our impulses without acting out is a new freedom. Over time, the desire to act against our values begins to fade.

Our self-made prisons no longer serve us. We are free to explore and discover what we are good at. We are free to participate, create, care and share, surprise ourselves, take risks, be vulnerable, and stand on our own two feet. We find our beliefs and begin to act on them. We make decisions based on our values. We walk through fear and wake up to the miracles that surround us. We are free to be who we are and live as we choose.

When we feel the deepest gratitude, we can look back and see that our path to that moment was neither short nor straight. What seemed like the worst decisions at one time in our recovery opened the door for some of our greatest opportunities later on. We may simply outgrow some of our decisions. What was right for us at one point in our recovery may not be right for the rest of our lives, but it can be difficult for us to move on. Gifts can come wrapped in such strange packages that we don't always recognize them when they arrive. Nothing that happens is entirely good or entirely bad. We do not pretend that there are no mistakes in recovery, but sometimes those mistakes can take us in a direction we hadn't thought of before.

Recovery is not a standardizing, "cookie-cutter" process. We don't all go through the process in the same way, and we don't all come out of it the same. But there are some familiar landmarks we pass. We have phases and stages, corners we turn, staircases we climb. Each of us has periods of intense growth and times when change is more subtle. Having a new way to live means that we have to live in new ways, and we can get confused or lost even when we have many years clean. Allowing each other room to grow at our own pace is difficult, especially when we care for each other, but self-acceptance and self-respect are the result of going through the process in our own way.

Time is not the same as experience. Just because we have been here for a long time doesn't mean that we know everything we need to know. We don't graduate from the simple steps that keep us clean and free. Our lives continue to unfold. We start at different places and we grow at different paces. Time represents the opportunity for growth, but we still have to step up to the challenge and be open to the lessons. Practicing honesty, open-mindedness, and willingness keeps us teachable, grateful, and humble. The difference between humility and humiliation can be the level of acceptance we have about the information we get. When we listen with an open mind, anyone can carry a message to us.

There are no unnecessary principles in NA, though we may learn them in our own time and in our own order. We can't expect to find what we are looking for if we work some of the steps and not others—or if we are ignoring the traditions, or living in conflict with our own values. Spiritual principles are not dependent on time or circumstance. We learn by observation and experience. There is a difference between feeling like we are so sick that we will never get better and knowing that we are never done growing or recovering. Exploration lasts a lifetime. We begin over and over. It gets easier to act in our own best interest, even when we are feeling resistant. A member shared, "I often hear newcomers say that they can't imagine going to NA meetings for the rest of their lives. I had the same reservation, but today I can't imagine my life without NA." We learn to do what we have to do, as well as what we want to do. We don't always want to work our program, but we know the rewards we get when we take responsibility for our recovery—and the consequences when we do not.

New information can be hard for us to accept when it doesn't come to us in the way we think it should. Whether the information itself is surprising or the messenger is not someone we usually look to for guidance, we may dismiss new ideas because we don't like the package. A member shared, "I would stand on my head in a corner if my sponsor told me it would work, but when the words that could save my life come from someone I really don't care for, it's easy to dismiss them." New tools are available to us when we allow ourselves to be surprised by both the message and the messenger. If it brings us to reevaluate our belief system, so much the better—we can see our initial resistance as a reservation in our willingness. Trying new things in recovery is one way we keep ourselves from getting stuck. No matter how long we have been clean, we can go to meetings and listen for the music. "It's like when your ears pop," a member shared. "Suddenly, I could hear what I didn't know I was missing before."

Our traditions teach us that in NA there are no classes of membership. It follows that the new member is as likely to save the life of the oldtimer as the reverse. When we stay open to that reality, many of the limitations we set for ourselves disappear. We teach by example. Even when we are teaching what not to do, we are still carrying a message. Sharing our experience gives it meaning and value. Our hope is that the next member will do better than we did, that they can learn from our mistakes. It doesn't always work: We are people who tend to learn things the hard way. But when a member with two years clean shares with us that the experience we had at ten years clean kept them from doing the same thing, we know that we are getting better, personally and as a fellowship.

Wisdom is building on past experience to cope with new events. When we think about our lives now in contrast to our active addiction, it is important to remember that "it is not where we have been that counts, but where we are going." But where we have been in recovery is the foundation of our wisdom. We learn from our experience, and we use it to help others. Our wisdom grows as we learn to see ourselves honestly, without judging or jumping to conclusions.

Growing Pains

Sooner or later, we experience a particular kind of opportunity or catastrophe we haven't heard about in meetings. Sometimes an event like a breakup, the loss of a job, or changes in our family triggers a flow of feelings, and it doesn't stop. Grief, hardship, or betrayal can make us feel terribly lonely. Occasionally, we experience physical changes that bring emotional freight with them, including depression, anxiety, and deep fear.

There are also times when we find ourselves in crisis even though the circumstances of our lives look pretty good. Even the excitement of living our dreams—taking on a new career, moving to a faraway place, creating a family—can make us feel like we don't belong. Sometimes an outside event starts the ball rolling. At other times a cascade of emotions seems to start from nowhere. It can feel like we are backed into a corner, even if nothing is really happening at all. Once we have been through this feeling and survived it clean, we know it won't last forever. But that doesn't mean we can see our way out. We come through these experiences with a deepened understanding and faith in our recovery. Through hard work and grace, if we keep coming back, we do get free.

Eventually all of us come to an emotional crisis in recovery. We start wondering if recovery will last, or if we had just gotten a brief reprieve and we are about to go crazy again. A member shared, "My life seemed stable by outward appearances, but inside I was a mess. I was clean, but miserable, reactive, and fearful." We find ourselves in these dark places sometimes with many, many years clean. We deal with our addiction, but some of our underlying issues remain untouched. Long-buried emotions come pouring to the surface, and we may or may not have the tools to deal with them. "As I discovered things about myself," a member shared, "my emotions started to run amok." There are no bitter ends in recovery, but sometimes it feels like that's where we are. Recovery gives us a new chance at life. Sometimes we have to accept that invitation more than once.

The bottoms we hit in recovery can be frightening. We go through some dark times; when we are in pain, it can be hard to reach out, and easier to see differences. But even in the darkness the process is still going on. When NA members say, "Don't give up five minutes before the miracle," we're not just talking about the first one. Our lives are full of moments when we are faced with the difficult decision to grow or go. Many of us leave not when things are horrible, but when we have one more spiritual hump to get over. We lose our way right before the miracle—sometimes again and again.

The faith that leads us to build a successful life may not be sufficient to sustain that day after day. A new kind of surrender is necessary if we are to stay clean and keep growing. Spiritual growth can be bewildering, frightening, and very lonely. Some of us give up on the process at this crucial point when there is nothing left to blame or change but ourselves. Selfishness and self-centeredness die hard. But we can get through it with the help of others who have survived this passage, and we find great gifts are waiting for us on the other side. What we heard when we were new still stands: Keep coming back, no matter what! Many of the challenges we face have concrete symptoms, but are actually spiritual in nature. It's hard to spot a spiritual crisis: Usually it is disguised as a crisis in our relationships, finances, career, or family.

When we are in crisis we may try all kinds of escapes and excuses before we resort to the steps. We can be intolerant, angry, defensive, vengeful, guilty, and resentful, testing the patience and tolerance of those around us. The only way out is through. We must roll up our sleeves and get to work. These struggles often push us into to the next phase in our recovery. We can come out stronger and healthier people for the experience, if we are willing to do the work.

Early in recovery we were told that if we kept coming to meetings, sooner or later we would hear our story. It would be a mistake to think that our using story is the only one we need to listen for. Our recovery story is no less dramatic, and there are times when we need just as much to go to meetings and listen for that. We hear it when we learn to listen with our heart as well as our ears. Sometimes we have to go looking for it, seeking new meetings, asking around, and sharing about what's going on. We find people who have been through what we're going through, and got through it clean. We need other people to walk us through hard times, and we need to reach out and help others as we heal.

There is hope. When we listen to others share their pain and how they get through it, we get a broader view. We see new tools in action, and we can learn to use their experience to go forward in our own lives. When we change our attitude or perspective, we can find a new sense of compassion and gratitude. Perhaps the most valuable lesson of all is empathy. However, empathy isn't a treatment plan; it's a way of life. When we can relate with one another and see each other's growth, we begin to believe in the possibility of our own recovery. Listening to other addicts share without judging them is the beginning of listening to our own heart without judgment or punishment. When we have compassion for ourselves, we give ourselves permission to be in the world, and that makes us much more useful to the world.

Our ability to feel joy and gratitude can be a direct result of the suffering we have endured. Staying clean is not a guarantee that nothing bad will happen, but the principles in the steps teach us how to live on life's terms and give us the courage, strength, and wisdom to stay clean no matter what. We are able to live lives of joy and purpose no matter what we have been through. Faith is what keeps us doing the footwork even when we can't see the reason.

One of the benefits of reaching out is finding that our most painful experiences can help someone else. When we say, "I've been through that, and I stayed clean," we realize with gratitude that we have gotten to the other side of something we had feared we could not get through. There is great satisfaction in being able not just to look back, but to reach back and help someone else across.

Getting through hard times strengthens our faith. When we are grappling with issues that don't have easy answers, we experience our greatest growth. One member suggested,

"There are spiritual tourists and spiritual explorers; one plays it very safe, and the other will step right out there and try God out. We get more certain of that relationship as we go." As we mature in recovery, we learn to be comfortable with the hard questions rather than only feeling okay when we think we've settled them. Having all the answers makes it hard to be teachable. Often when we say we are looking for solutions, what we are really seeking is control. Over and over we go looking for the answers, but there really aren't that many to find—and we don't need that many. The steps help us to increase our ability to be honest with ourselves and others. More often, and sooner in the process, we are able to recognize our responsibility for our actions and motives. Identifying what drives us to act as we do helps us to find relief from all the ways our disease shows up. It also gives us the ability to see more clearly. We begin to move toward what we want rather than just away from what we fear.

Each time we let go, there is a degree of mourning and then an opening of possibility. Each time we get through that process we find new freedom in ourselves. But it can take years to let go enough to feel that freedom. We hang on fiercely, mistaking the attempt to control all the variables in our lives for vigilance in our recovery. Letting go looks different at different times in our recovery.

Making peace with loss is one way we learn acceptance. When we experience loss and find that we can still feel complete within ourselves, something changes. The feeling that we must constantly fight for our survival starts to ease. We can let someone else be right, or let something go, without losing ourselves or our dignity. We can see our part in situations without falling into the belief that everything has to be somebody's fault. Often, a loss we are struggling to accept in the present helps us to deal with earlier losses that haunt us. Acceptance is not an all-or-nothing event, and it doesn't necessarily happen all at once. Like so many lessons in recovery, there are less painful ways to learn, but they're not always the ones that stay with us.

The more we learn about ourselves, the more we are able to work toward our own personal vision of hope. At the same time, we remember that our vision for ourselves is a fleeting glimpse of our Higher Power's will for us. As we pursue our dreams, we may find ourselves in places we never imagined. It's all possible, but that means we take risks and sometimes experience failure. Even when we fall flat on our face, we can get up again and move forward. That's part of the journey, too. We get less and less afraid of the truth. But we don't get there by standing still and waiting for recovery to happen to us. We learn, we grow, we give, we create—and we keep coming back.

A Vision of Hope

Learning about acceptance, love, and compassion helps us to accept ourselves without conditions. As our faith deepens, our understanding of what it means to act in good faith changes as well. We no longer use our disease or where we are in our recovery as an alibi for bad behavior. Our recovery is constantly enriched by what we learn. We make peace with ourselves—with all we have gained, and lost, and learned, and become. We find gratitude for the events that bring us to this moment. The process is a power greater than ourselves. The reward for staying with it is feeling at peace with who we are.

Self-acceptance changes over time. We learn to live with our frailties and imperfections. We find that the defects we accept and forgive are more likely to be removed than those we fight against and try to control. We can mistake the obstacles in our path for a part of ourselves. Learning to direct our attention toward our assets and goals and away from our defects and obsessions is a new freedom. We start to believe that our positive attributes are not part of a façade or a figment of our imagination. Our feelings don't frighten us like they used to, and they seem to pass more quickly. We know that we may not change our feelings right away, but we can change our behavior. Mood follows action. When we do the right thing, we can start to feel better.

The person we see in the mirror may bear little resemblance to the version of ourselves that other people know. When we are locked in self-obsession, we may have no idea of the damage we are doing to the people around us, or even to ourselves. Similarly, when we reach out, we may not see the positive effects we have on our own spirits or the world around us. We may still see ourselves as we were when we got here, not recognizing that the principles we have been practicing have become part of who we are. We trust our sponsors and friends to show us the changes we cannot see in ourselves.

Caring for our spiritual condition is like cleaning the house: If we want the benefit, the work must be ongoing. The better we do at keeping up with the daily routines, the less painful the big cleaning is when it comes, and the less often we have to undertake a major overhaul. We are responsible for our recovery, but that doesn't have to be an endless chore. A member shared, "There was a time when I dreaded stepwork. It felt like a punishment. Now I am excited to work on my recovery, because I know the steps are the road to freedom."

It's not recovery that is painful; our resistance to it is what hurts. When we step away from our recovery and act against our beliefs—that hurts. Using is about distortion. We are drawn to things that distort our perception, from drug use to resentment. Sanity is living in harmony with reality. When we are spiritually awake, we are willing to see clearly. We recognize the habits of mind that lead us back to the same feelings over and over, regardless of what's happening around us. Until we stamp it with the name "excitement" or "fear," the feeling can be identical. Making a choice in how we describe our experience gives us a choice in how we experience our lives.

Allowing ourselves to be happy can be a surprisingly long process. It always continues in one way or another. Some of us fear contentment because it might lead to complacency. Others of us fear that if we are ever content, there will be nothing left to try for. Learning what truly makes us happy can be hard, especially if our relationship to seeking pleasure was tangled up with our most destructive behavior. Finding the balance is a challenge. "When I got clean I could feel the grief of every leaf falling from the tree," a member shared. "I feel like a novice at finding joy. I thought I would have to let go of pleasure to be clean."

What we learn about love in the rooms prepares us for other kinds of relationships. We may find love, create families, or be restored to the families we had left behind. Some of us discover that we have talents for contributing to the world in other ways, whether through our creativity, our empathy, or our addict ability to focus on one thing and do it 'til it's done. The skills we learn in the rest of our lives, in turn, become tools we use to help carry the message. When we stay involved with NA, we can see that we have a valuable contribution to make to the world. We may not see all these changes at first, but we feel it somehow and get a glimmer of hope that our lives are changing.

Desperation to Passion

Once the process of cleaning up the wreckage begins, the ways that we need to grow may not be visible from the outside. We go from being totally impulsive to feeling like our decisions have to be permanent. Something has to drive us or draw us. We need a purpose, or we start entertaining ourselves with obsession and compulsion. There is something about being stuck that feels hopeless, and easily turns into complacency and indifference. It can feel wrong or embarrassing to be struggling to keep the light on in our own recovery when we think we are supposed to be carrying the message to others. The responsibility we feel to carry a message can serve as an excuse not to share the truth about our lives. But without the truth, we have no message at all. And when we are not open, it's hard for light to get in. Admitting is the beginning of change.

Putting the life back in our recovery is really not that hard. We look for the passion, and we nurture it. The hard part is finding the willingness to take action and pick up the phone or go to a meeting when we are feeling uninspired. There is magic and a healing grace in meetings, but we cannot see it when our attitude blinds us. Coming back to meetings after we have been gone for a while can be awkward and difficult, or it can be like coming home. There is a sweetness to walking into a room we have not been in for some time and seeing so much unchanged. Still, meetings make more sense when we attend them regularly. When we drift in and out, they can seem dull and boring. Part of the magic comes from continuity: seeing each other grow and change, watching the miracle unfold in one another's lives. Occasionally someone shares brilliant words. More often the brilliance is in what we see, not what we hear.

Passion is a lot like desperation: It is a motivating, energizing force that can propel us forward. But passion is rarely bestowed on us; it comes from within. The more we draw on our passion, the more of it we have. Making the shift from desperation to passion is a First Step issue. Our journey is always just beginning, and our capacity—and our need—for spiritual growth is infinite. The same tools that brought us from the brink of death can continue to bring us miracles beyond measure when we learn to fuel our journey with passion and excitement, rather than pain and desperation.

There is a transition that happens to each of us in the process of recovery, an indefinable moment when we move from desperation to passion. Where we had been motivated by the fear of greater pain, we start to see new opportunities for growth in our struggles, and become willing to move forward out of hope, rather than fear. This may not be our first spiritual awakening, but it is clearly an awakening of the spirit into a new sense of possibility.

Faith in the process means believing that we are moving in the right direction, even if it's not where we thought we would be going. We take on greater challenges, we stand for principles we never had before, we tend to our responsibilities even when they seem too heavy to bear. We learn that our Higher Power will help us do what we cannot—but will not do for us what we can do for ourselves. It is surprising to find how much we actually can handle. When we stop trying to control things we are powerless over, we learn where our power truly lies, and how we can use that to make changes in ourselves and our world.

We are a part of something today. But we are not just part of one thing: What we learn about unity in NA helps us to figure out how to be members of our families, members of our communities, members of a team at work or at play. We learn that we are never alone: We are here with one another and for one another. We trust that more and more as our experience grows. We can see that our actions have consequences for us and for the people around us. Denying this is a form of self-obsession. We do matter, and we want to consider how we contribute.

Each time we surrender, we find once more that the desperation that drives us to our knees fuels the passion that carries us forward. When hope manifests into reality, our lives change. Our experience affirms what we believe, and belief grows into faith. When our faith grows into knowledge, the program that we once struggled to practice has become part of who we are. We find here what we were looking for all along: connection to others, connection to a Higher Power, connection to the world around us—and, most surprising of all, connection to ourselves.

Why We Stay

What is it that keeps us in NA after the initial desperation eases? Of course, there's the desire to help the newcomer; our Twelfth Step reminds us that this must always come first. But many of us, at some point in our recovery, have felt that perhaps that was all that was left in the rooms for us. Our commitment to help might have kept us coming back, but some of us were left with a nagging feeling that we hesitated to share: "Is this really all there is?"

Our answer today is a resounding "No." In our lives and in the lives of addicts around the world, we can see change—not only from the desperate, lonely people we were when we got here. We can see great changes in ourselves and in the way we relate to others from the first time we work the steps compared to our next pass, and our next. Our experience in NA service teaches us to interact with others in environments that are sometimes stressful, and to remain loving and open even as we stand our ground. We learn when it's important to stand for principles, and when it's best to step aside in the name of unity, knowing that a loving God is ultimately in charge. We plan for the future just for today and let go of the outcome, even when we really want it. Living, loving, surviving loss, and celebrating success, we find that the tools of recovery that gave us our lives also help us to live with grace, integrity, and joy. As we practice principles, our understanding grows and deepens.

There is no limit to the process. There are no limits to where our recovery can take us, no limits to how much better we can get. We short-circuit our recovery when we keep a reservation in our Second Step by thinking that there are some parts of who we are that cannot be restored. When we accept the possibility that we can get infinitely better—that there is no end to what recovery has to offer—we begin to understand that spirituality is not just a way out. It is a way of life that will continue to bring us new gifts, new possibilities, and new awareness as long as we practice it. If we allow ourselves to be motivated not by fear of the past but by hope for the future, we are as excited to move forward when life is good as we are when we are struggling.

We have found a way in—to life, to freedom, to passion, to limitless growth. We are no longer trapped in a process driven by our own desperation. Something different happens as we move into recovery motivated by passion, hope, and excitement. We are released into our own lives. We are freed from the feeling that we must constantly be on guard. We are free to discover the capacity of our own hearts: Where we have been closed down, we have the ability to love and care for others more deeply than we had imagined.

Yes, we are a vision of hope, as the Basic Text says. This book is about seeing that hope as something that always grows, drawing us forward throughout our recovery and throughout our lives. We don't just recover; we thrive. The NA program gives us tools for living. The work is never-ending, and the rewards of living the program are ongoing as well. We work to improve our circumstances, creating and re-creating a life that matches our vision for ourselves. Often the change we seek is in our ideas and attitudes. We learn to see the world more clearly. We are so grateful for the recovery we can see in ourselves and the people around us. Great rewards are always waiting for us, if we are willing to make the effort.

Narcotics Anonymous is a bridge to life, and a path we can walk throughout our lives. The gift is freedom. Each level of freedom we experience opens us to greater freedom beyond, just as each level of awareness allows us to recognize how much we do not yet see. Although we may live very differently from one another, we share the same journey. We are so grateful to have found recovery, to be living clean, and to know, wherever we are in our travels—the journey continues.

The Ties That Bind

Narcotics Anonymous is a program of action, not theory. We don't think our way into a new way of living; we live our way into a new way of thinking. Before we got clean, our identity was built on fantasy: who we could be, would be, should be, or even who we used to be. In recovery we connect with reality through action. We show up and do our part. We experiment with jobs, relationships, and service commitments. Some of us begin simply by trying to keep a houseplant alive. Wherever we start, each of us ventures out into the world—clean—and tries something new. We learn who we are by taking a stand, taking risks, and allowing ourselves to be vulnerable. Even when we make mistakes, we can learn something vital about ourselves.

We identify as addicts, and the principle of anonymity teaches us that this is the most important thing. If we forget we have a deadly disease, it doesn't really matter who or what else we think we are. But once we are clear about that, and get used to the idea of being clean, all kinds of possibilities open up to us. As recovering addicts, we are free to explore the world and to consider who we are and who we want to become. An experienced member suggested that the whole trick to living is figuring out who we are and doing it on purpose.

Connection to Ourselves

It can take a long time to set ourselves free. When we come to recovery we have been devastated in many ways. Although living clean isn't all about crisis, it can sometimes seem that way. Our feelings are so powerful. There is so much change in our lives, and change can be messy even when it's positive. Our personalities and our sense of who we are were warped by our addiction, and when we get clean we are even more confused. It can be a while before we have the opportunity (or the need) to ask, "Okay. Who am I now?" We change in recovery, but we also uncover who we were all along. We find ourselves. For many of us, this is the restoration the Second Step talks about. It may even be a restoration to a state we've never experienced before, because we've never had the chance to be ourselves without pretending, without hiding, without trying to be something else.

There may be many different ways we describe ourselves, and the ones that seem most important can change depending on where we are in our lives. Identity is a confusing word. It indicates the things that make us different from each other, and the things that make us exactly the same. Our identity is composed of the things that distinguish us either as part of a group or as separate from it. We are as different as our stories, but our literature reminds us that "addiction makes us one of a kind."

At some point, our identity as using addicts came to define us. At the end of the road, it seemed like we were nothing but our addiction. As we stay clean, we begin to discover who we are. Some of us return to an identity we once knew and had lost; others of us come into the process uncertain of who we might be. Experiences from our past can make it hard for some of us to see ourselves in new ways. The labels we have applied to ourselves don't allow us to change. Powerful emotional experiences can shape our identity; sometimes they seem to define us. Those experiences made us who we are, and we embrace them. For that matter, we might not want to see ourselves otherwise. Sometimes we are simply stuck in unresolved past experiences like abuse, prison, or the death of someone we love. How do we reconcile who we have been with who we are becoming in recovery? We want to be free of our past without missing any opportunities to learn from it.

Sometimes it can take a while for our sense of ourselves to catch up to who we are. We may even sabotage ourselves to return to familiar chaos or pain when our lives start seeming too different from what they had been. Gradually, we learn that much of the unmanageability we struggle with is the result of the choices we make. When we begin to get comfortable with new choices, our lives change—sometimes radically.

What makes us happiest are things it may never have occurred to us to want. Some of us have the experience of "lost dreams awakening," picking up our desires where we left them and finally living the lives we had always wanted. Others of us find that the dreams we left behind no longer fit the people we have become. We come in with a regrettable history of broken promises and broken dreams, of dishonesty, betrayal, and failure. Believing we are worthy of the things we want can be its own process. We may have been afraid to dream at all. Some of us punish ourselves in recovery for years, holding ourselves back from joy because we feel we don't deserve it. The tools and the love we find in NA can help us break these patterns, no matter how long we have been living with them.

We can get stuck in patterns so quickly. Vigilance is necessary to keep old patterns from resurfacing. Something needs to break the circuit of our negative thinking. It may be an action we take, like meditating or going to a meeting; it may be an action someone else takes. Our friends and sponsors come to know us well enough to recognize when we are off course, and help us to make a shift. When we are living just for today, we find courage that we never expected, and we can go forward into our lives with joy, excitement, and great hope for what is possible. But when we dwell in the past or worry about the future, we find ourselves trapped again almost before we know what happened.

There is no single, easy answer to how we make peace with our past, and it rarely happens all at once. Throughout our recovery, different pieces of ourselves become available to us, and other parts are ready to be let go. Sometimes this is a peaceful process, and sometimes it's terrifying. The fact that something does not get resolved in one round of steps or in a few conversations with our sponsor does not mean we are not progressing. Returning again and again, in stepwork or in dreams, to "the scene of the crime" is part of the experience many of us share in recovery. Each step we work gives us back a piece of ourselves and relieves a little of our burden of regret, shame, and fear. We let go of some things we believed about ourselves and find others. We return to some of the things we once cherished and find out if they still suit us today. The ways we change can be surprising.

We leave pieces behind along the way. It is almost like a children's game: With each step forward, we must turn around and retrieve a piece of our past. Defects of character are removed, but other things are as well. We change jobs and find out how much our identity was tied up in what we did for a living, or we experience a change in our relationship and find that it changes us in other ways as well. This can be upsetting. We may not want to admit that what worked for us yesterday is no longer in our best interest. As we start to know ourselves, we may be afraid to keep growing because it opens up the possibility that we might lose the self we have only just gotten to know. Experience teaches us that the more willing we are to move forward in our lives, the more fully we become ourselves.

We learn what is true for us by going through difficulty, staying clean, and looking back on the experience. We may think we are the ones being tested, but the reality is that we are continually testing our faith and understanding against our experience. When we go through difficulty in recovery, it can feel like we are in the same place we were before we got clean. And while sometimes we re-create old experiences in our new lives, more often we mistake a temporary difficulty for a permanent condition.

The simple act of accepting ourselves changes us. We start treating ourselves better and we respond to the world with a new humility. The Basic Text says in the Eighth Step, "We want to look the world in the eye with neither aggressiveness nor fear." As we clean up our wreckage and live differently, we can respect our actions and find respect for ourselves in the process. Part of the charm of many of our more experienced members is that they can seem so eccentric. One suggested that this was a consequence of no longer having defenses in the way. More and more, we are comfortable just being ourselves. We appear in the world exactly as we are. That freedom is part of the promise of our Third Tradition. Because we have only one requirement for membership—the desire to stop using—we are given permission to be who we are. We no longer have to lie to gain acceptance.

Connection to a Higher Power

Many of us notice when we first come to meetings that members who are recovering and happy with themselves seem to shine. That light of the spirit is the most beautiful thing we have to offer, and it's less fragile than we think. After all, it survived our addiction! Tending that light is partly about nurturing the passion inside us, and partly a process of trimming away all the stuff that hides us from ourselves. Our defects "grow in the dark." In the light of recovery, our assets begin to blossom.

There is more than one way we understand the phrase "practicing these principles." We practice, and we don't always get it right. The Basic Text tells us in the Sixth Step, "We learn that we are growing when we make new mistakes..." Regular practice, beginning with the basics and gradually progressing from there, is exactly how we get good at anything, from learning to play an instrument or speak a new language to learning how to live a spiritual, principled, and rewarding life. We are not just learning new skills; we are breaking old habits. Some are so deeply ingrained that they feel like a part of who we are.

Building a relationship with something greater than ourselves is a project we undertake the first time we approach the steps, and it continues throughout our recovery. For some of us, spiritual disciplines, including prayer and meditation, shape our day. Others of us try to live our lives as a prayer, offering all of our actions as gifts to our Higher Power. However we practice or experience it, our relationship with our Higher Power comes to shape our understanding of who we are and how we relate to the world around us. Our actions and motives reflect our values and beliefs. When we are in tune with a power greater than ourselves, we seem to flow more easily with the currents in our lives.

After years clean, we experience ourselves differently than we did in the beginning. As we develop an identity beyond "addict," we wonder whether that label still applies, whether we still belong in the fellowship. We tend to learn balance by bouncing off both extremes. Questioning our relationship with NA can take it to a deeper level. The answers we find help to resolve our new reservations, and the security to question our foundation is part of the secret to solidifying it for a lifetime.

It is said that those wishing to discover a new land must spend a long time at sea. Sometimes when we feel like we are lost at sea, we may wonder whether the program still matters for us. We are afraid to doubt because we know it can kill us, but the fear of questioning our new way of life can lead us to be dishonest with ourselves. NA isn't about learning to be compliant; it's about establishing a relationship with something greater than ourselves, and often that relationship can be a little stormy. It is important to know there are members who will give us space to question our recovery, but don't quite let go of us, either. Though some people will be unsure how to respond to our doubt, sharing our feelings can help us to see that we are not alone. In moments of extreme uncertainty, "fake it 'til ya make it" is exactly the wrong prescription, even though it may work just fine at other times. We need to be brutally honest with ourselves about what we feel and what we believe. Out of these moments of doubt can grow a faith that is truly our own. We can neither deny nor indulge these feelings; they must be handled with care.

We learn what is true for us, and that sets the direction for our lives. Our moral compass is the product of the work we do to understand and apply spiritual principles. When we move away from what we know is right, we feel frustrated and trapped. When we forget what is true for us, we lose our way and drift dangerously. On the other hand, when our understanding of the truth is changing, we may feel much more lost than we actually are. That compass is very much at work and is leading us in a new direction. Through these periods of grave doubt and uncertainty, we find a new surrender, a deeper faith, and often a very different sense of who we are.

We run back to our old ways for fear that we may become someone we don't recognize or won't even like. Some of us fear that if we go all the way inside, what we will find is... nothing. But the emptiness we once feared gives us space for growth and change. We stop trying so hard to re-create ourselves and simply allow it to happen. As we work our way through those layers, we find safety, clarity, and confidence that no matter what happens, we don't have to lose ourselves again.

There are some questions we can only answer alone, but in order to face those questions alone, we need the support of people we trust. The difference between solitude and isolation is another fine line we identify through experience. One question we learn to ask ourselves is "Am I acting in the service of a greater good right now?" We may need to be alone to connect with our Higher Power. Sometimes the best thing we can do is to rest and unwind, read a book or watch a movie, and let go. This is not the same as isolation—though the difference may not be apparent to anyone else. The difference is inside. We come to identify for ourselves what is restorative time alone and what is destructive withdrawal.

Acceptance of our changing spirituality is part of our personal evolution. If our relationship with a Higher Power is real and meaningful, of course it will change over time. But sometimes this feels like a crisis. If we surrender, it drives us back to the steps, and in revisiting Steps Two and Three we can find a relationship to faith that makes more sense to us. As our values change, our beliefs are likely to develop as well. Letting go of the idea that we have to understand why things happen or how it all works frees us to have a spiritual experience without wondering if we're doing it right.

Action is not always visible. Sometimes in order for us to move forward we must stand very still. Meditation can be hard because it can be so uncomfortable to be quiet with ourselves, to simply stand in the moment and be present. But this is where we ask for help, listen for answers, look ourselves in the eye, and see who we are, where we are, and how we are. When we can be still and observe without judgment, we are given the clarity to see what is right for us and what is not.

We learn to trust our process and allow it the time it needs to work. When we set timelines for how "well" we should be, or how long we will grieve, be afraid, or not know the answer to a question, we can set ourselves up to believe that recovery isn't working. Recovery works very well, but not always on the schedule we set for it. There is no substitute for time.

A lot of the stepwork we do after the first time through is about clarity: listening to the voice within that tells us when what we are doing is right, and when it's not in line with our values. Each time, we release more of what ties us to false expectations and beliefs about who we are. We are no longer contained by our addiction or our old, narrow view of what life is "supposed" to look like. We learn that the power we gain in the Eleventh Step is available to us when we are doing our Higher Power's will and living in self-acceptance. The biggest changes in recovery often happen when we're not looking. We wake up and find ourselves in lives we hardly recognize as our own. We find stability, dignity, and honor in our dealings with others where once we saw struggle, degradation, and alienation.

We gain self-respect when we follow through on commitments. These may begin with group service commitments: making coffee, chairing a meeting, and so forth. As our ability to follow through begins to grow, we take on larger challenges. Perhaps the biggest one is following through on our commitment to work the steps. One of our members suggests that it's not just the work we do in the steps, but the way we work the steps that sets the pattern for our lives. Taking on a big project in little pieces, working consistently on something that is important even when it is hard or unpleasant, teaches us different things than we learn by pushing through in a rush or working all night to meet a deadline.

Through the steps, we peel back the layers of illusion that we mistake for ourselves. We learn that we have a disease, but that our disease isn't all we are. We learn that we are not God. We learn that we are not our past or our defects of character. We notice when we are confusing *how* we are for *who* we are. As we work our way deeper and deeper through the illusions, some of us wonder what will be left.

We talk to members we respect and trust, and they remind us that working a program is not going to turn us into anyone other than who we truly are. As we develop a conscious contact with a Power greater than ourselves, we grow into the awareness that our Higher Power doesn't want an imaginary, idealized version of us. We come as we are, and we serve best when we are most fully ourselves. The simple act of being present without trying to pretend works to peel away the distortions and lies, our defects, our baggage, and our nagging sense of inadequacy. We learn who we are precisely when we forget ourselves in service to others.

Connection to the World Around Us

We build our foundation in recovery. As we become more secure, we broaden our horizons and accomplish goals we would never have considered before. Many of us go back to school, pursue careers, and start families. We come back regularly to check our foundation for cracks and shifting, and to reinforce it where needed. Such a sturdy foundation would not be necessary if we were just pitching a tent, but we build skyscrapers on our foundations. Those skyscrapers must be securely grounded so that renovating one room doesn't cause the entire structure to collapse.

The tools we use to build our foundation are not the only tools we need later on. It's not that they lose their value. The basics are always important—but at some point they may not be enough to sustain us. When we arrive at a moment when everything we know is not enough for us, we turn to members with more experience. We are likely to get the same simple guidance we have heard from the beginning: The answers are in the steps. A deeper relationship with the steps continues to develop even after we have worked them many times. For some of us, consistent practices of prayer, meditation, writing, or physical exercise are useful in the beginning but grow richer over time. The simple fact of having maintained a practice for a long time offers a structure for our program that we can depend on.

For many of us, getting and staying clean is our greatest accomplishment, no matter what else we do in life. For others, it is the most beautiful gift we have been given. It is not always possible for us to share the thing for which we are most grateful with people outside recovery. That may feel like a little barrier between us and the world.

Some of us stay entirely within the sphere of recovery: All of our friends are in recovery, our whole world is tied up with the fellowship—not because we are afraid to venture out, but because we derive so much satisfaction from the rich interactions we have in NA. The way we share, this level of deep identification that makes NA feel so special to us—talking openly about feelings, finding humor in some of the darkest, most frightening things that have happened to us—is not always available outside the rooms.

For some of us, that's fine. We are happy making our lives in NA. For others, creating outside the rooms the same kinds of intimacy and community that we have learned to love in recovery presents an exciting challenge. We may experience some kinds of connection in NA and other kinds in other places—with our families, religious communities, coworkers, or neighbors. We are comfortable having some of our identity here and some there. Each of us finds the blend that works for us, just for today. Self-acceptance, for most of us, means finding a balance between our recovery and our lives outside NA.

There are times when we are not around the fellowship as much as we would like to be. We notice the difference in our recovery; we may also notice the difference in how it feels when we come back. When we are not as closely connected, it's easy to feel left out. People ask where we've been and we take offense. We can be in grave danger when we start feeling angry at meetings because people are not responding to us the way we like.

The tools of this program can become weapons if we choose to use them that way. Even our stepwork can become an opportunity for us to abuse ourselves about our imperfections. Some members say that our defects are just survival mechanisms that stopped working. Likewise, our best tools sometimes grow from our worst defects of character. We swing from self-obsession to intensive work on our recovery and gradually find a balance between these extremes, spending more time closer to the center as we practice.

When we hit our thumb with a hammer, our sense of proportion changes and it feels like our thumb is enormous. We think about every movement in relation to that thumb and whether anything might touch it. The same is true of our egos. When we are damaged or hurt in some way, we feel larger than life. Every conversation seems to be about us. Humility is about discovering a sense of proportion firmly grounded in reality. We gain a better perspective on how much space we actually occupy. We discover that we are neither as big nor as small as we might think. We are important in the lives of the people around us, but that doesn't mean they are always thinking about how their actions will affect us.

Self-obsession is rooted in fear. One of the deepest fears many of us share is that we will lose ourselves entirely. We are afraid to let go of what we know about ourselves in order to change, afraid to let go of our sense of ourselves in the world in order to meditate, afraid to let go of our beliefs about our place in the world for fear we will never fit anywhere. For many of us, letting ourselves go may be the first step toward finding ourselves. We don't have to hold on so tight. One of our members shares that "when I turn it over but don't let go, I'm just upside-down." Letting go gives us the freedom to right ourselves again, naturally and gradually, rather than forcing ourselves into a mold of how we think we ought to be.

We struggle with self-obsession throughout our lives. This is not a defect we let go of just once. It comes up again and again. Often a feeling will send us into self-obsession. Addiction is a disease that distorts ideas and attitudes. When we practice acceptance, we distance ourselves from our reactions and reflexes. This gives us the ability to see more of the picture than our limited point of view allows. The Serenity Prayer is a tool we use again and again in our recovery: Considering what we can change and what we cannot becomes increasingly powerful.

Connection to Others

Some days it seems really easy to identify with others, to feel welcomed and welcoming in a meeting. At other times, all we hear are the things that set us apart from the group. When we start noticing the differences more than appreciating our similarities, it's usually a red flag indicating discomfort with ourselves. When we focus on the personalities of others, we may gossip, bicker, and contribute to disunity. When we focus on our own personality, we quickly become self-centered and self-obsessed. When we focus on living the will of our Higher Power and carrying the message, our identities grow and flourish. The Tenth Step offers us ample opportunity to tend to that development, nurturing the growth we want to encourage and pruning back the wayward branches before they grow out of control.

When we attend meetings regularly, people get to know us and see us over time. When a fellow member can point out to us, "You know, you always get depressed at this time of year," we can take action to address a pattern we could not see ourselves. When someone we don't know that well points out our generosity or loving kindness, we learn that people see goodness in us that perhaps we don't see in ourselves. Our fellows reflect us back to ourselves and show us how we have changed.

Practicing compassion helps us to stop comparing ourselves to others. We start seeing the deep connections and similarities between us. Our traditions teach us that we are all equal. This doesn't mean we are the same; our differences are striking and sometimes very entertaining. Many of us have shared that part of what made us feel comfortable in our earliest meetings is that there are so many different kinds of people in a single meeting, sharing and appearing friendly with one another. This can contrast sharply with what we have experienced before, in or out of active addiction.

The things that separate us in the outside world don't matter in NA. The disease does not discriminate, and neither should we. We know this is true in principle, but it is sometimes a struggle in practice. Some patterns of prejudice and discrimination are so deeply woven into the fabric of our lives that we don't even notice them. On the other hand, if we have had a lifetime of experience dealing with oppression or discrimination, we may be so conscious of its signs that we see it even where it doesn't exist.

For some of us, "hearing our story" or identifying is all about finding someone who shares our background or beliefs. Not experiencing that right away can be frustrating or frightening. "I can see it works," some of us have said, "but not for someone like me." When other members tell us our need for that companionship is overstated, we don't feel welcomed—we feel even more invisible. However, many of us have found that despite our initial discomfort, we do thrive in a diverse fellowship. We notice at first that we need addicts who share and understand our sexual identity or our heritage, for example; later we find that we need even more to have members around us who really understand us, no matter what we share. We may be surprised by the members whose stories we relate to, or with whom we feel comfortable talking.

It's uncomfortable when we feel like "the only one of our kind" in a meeting, but that can give way to a larger sense of connection. We learn to accept and love who we are whether or not we feel like we "match" the people around us; we learn to identify with people on other levels, whereas before, we might not have even tried. Many of us come to keep an eye on the door, paying special attention to newcomers who might feel like "the only..." In many local NA communities, it has taken a few members who stick around through that sense of isolation to create a community that is large and diverse. One or two very young addicts in a meeting make that meeting feel safe for the next young person who walks in, and so on. We learn that what once felt like a reason to isolate is actually one more reason why it's important that we're here: We are each uniquely qualified to carry the message to the addict who sees him- or herself in us.

We never know what will make someone feel a connection with us. When we sense a connection based on our shared disease and shared recovery, the ways in which we differ from one another become enriching rather than limiting. As we meet more people, attend conventions and events out of town, and connect with other members in service or online, our circle in NA grows, and we find people who share our experience. But more surprisingly, we find people who share our feelings—and even our sense of connection and disconnection—where we might never have thought to look for them. When we share our experience honestly, we give others the opportunity to relate to us and connect with us in spite of any surface differences.

When we do the work of helping people get clean, something changes inside us. We discover the magic, the gift, when we see the light come on in someone's eyes. We learn to get out of our self-obsession. So many of our solutions are in service. We reap the rewards of our efforts as long as we keep coming back. The addict we reach out to in a moment of need may well be the person who saves our life later.

There's a lot to be said for old-fashioned Twelfth-Step work. We can get confused, and limit our outreach to members we know who have relapsed. We can be fearful of new people we don't know. Perhaps there is reason to be cautious: We're dangerous when we're using. We alibi out of caring by saying that we are making amends to ourselves: "I don't need all that drama in my life." But when we "protect ourselves" from the newcomer, we don't defend our lives from drama; we deprive ourselves of the opportunity to witness the miracle. Sometimes what a new person needs most is just not to be alone. Simply allowing someone to be with us as we go about our lives can be priceless.

We teach one another how to reach out. Just because someone did it for us doesn't mean that we automatically know how to reach out to someone new. Bringing a sponsee along on a Twelfth-Step call gives them an opportunity to learn, and keeps us from trying to do that alone. We learn to be in the presence of great pain without taking it in or taking it on.

We feel deeply and experience our emotions at great extremes. We dive into life face-first or hide under the covers, afraid to move. The price of growth for many of us is the awakening of more feelings than we know how to live with. It takes courage and humility to keep from shutting down again. Often, after the fact, we recognize that our negative thinking had cascaded. Perhaps we started with allowing a resentment to fester, and found gradually that we were less honest. Withholding the truth gave way to lying, and then sharing got harder, and so forth, until we found ourselves dealing with the consequences of a whole lot of bad behavior. Addiction and recovery are both progressive. We are very rarely standing still. We are almost always either getting better or getting sicker.

We define ourselves by our choices. The decision to have a family means leaving behind the independence we knew before; the decision not to have a family means that we must find other ways to feel connected to people, and so on. Tradition Seven tells us that everything has a price regardless of intent, and we find the profound truth in that as we move forward in our lives and our recovery. Every choice we make, good and bad, means there were options we left behind. We can get lost in infinite webs of "what if?" as we start thinking about our lives. The Fourth Step warns us about getting caught in the "binge of emotional sorrow" that can result. We come to see ourselves not as we were but as we are becoming. NA helps us to live with the consequences—and the benefits—of our transformation.

We all have experience starting over in our lives with new people, places, and things, stepping into a new way of life we don't quite understand. The desire to survive and feel fulfilled is not unique to us as addicts, but in recovery we begin with connection to others and work our way to basic safety. And perhaps it has to be this way. To believe that we can trust the love in our lives is challenging. Those really deep needs are the ones we believe won't be met. It begins with the amends process, the understanding that we can forgive and be forgiven, that we can take responsibility for our actions and make better choices.

Although our destinations may be different, our journeys are very similar. We travel through many different identities before we find self-acceptance. We propel ourselves by using the tools we all share. When we are derailed, we end up in much the same place. When we are moving forward by practicing spiritual principles, we may go to very different places in our lives, but if we relapse, we end up in a common predicament. That is what we share most of all: not where we are going, but where we come from—and how we move forward.

Together we rise to the point of freedom. We need one another to get there, and one of the most beautiful things we do in the fellowship is support one another in pursuit of our dreams. Sharing our hopes and our successes is as much a part of carrying our message as sharing our fears and difficulties. We have a message of hope to carry. It's a gift and an obligation. We may not relate exactly to one another's dreams, but we can relate to the hope, energy, and excitement of trying to realize them. We are inspired by one another's journeys. Being present to one another's growth gives us the tools and inspiration to move forward ourselves. But we also find we are able to stay put, follow through, and live the lives we create. Our recovery is something we can trust and believe in. New beginnings are possible anytime we are ready.

A Spiritual Path

The steps are a path to spiritual growth. There is no separation between the "spiritual part" and the rest of our program. Just as the facets of a diamond are not separate from the stone, the spiritual aspects of our program are not separate parts; they are perspectives on the whole. It's all spiritual. Our understanding of what that means may change over time.

Sometimes we think of spiritual principles as separate from the actions we need to take, but in fact they are connected. Spiritual principles give us a language through which we develop our values and learn to live by them. The principles describe our beliefs, our actions, and the reasons we act. Our relationship to the principles we practice is creative. We learn from day to day to use them in new ways, in new combinations, to better express who we are and to help the people around us. When we understand them better, we are able to act more consistently with what we believe. As we practice spiritual principles, we discover that this doesn't "make us spiritual" at all. Instead, we are awakening to what has been going on inside us our whole lives. Spirituality is our natural state.

Awakening to Our Spirituality

We are not the only people who have spiritual awakenings, but there is a particular awakening we experience as a result of working the steps: We awaken to our own spirituality. We are newly alive to the world around us. We see more clearly and feel more acutely—and that isn't always comfortable. Some of our members believe that the most important spiritual awakening occurs when we walk in the door of Narcotics Anonymous, and we spend the rest of our recovery trying to understand what happened. For others of us, awakening, like so much else in recovery, seems to happen in layers: "The fog pulled back to where I could see how much fog there was," said one. "Each time it pulls back, I see more on the horizon; I have a sense of how big it is and how much I still can't see. With a little luck, I'll be waking up more and more my whole life."

Some of us have awakened spiritually with an overwhelming sense of a power greater than ourselves. Others have shared a slow, gentle reviving of spiritual awareness, whether or not we ever experience a sense of a Higher Power. The discovery that others care about us can be a spiritual awakening. For the first time we recognize that *we matter*. Living according to principles leads us to humility—a greater awareness of our place in the world and our ability to live comfortably in it. We often hear at meetings, "The most important thing to understand about a Higher Power is that you ain't it!" Whatever it takes for us to realize that we are not the center of the universe, it's worth it. We may be too clever to declare ourselves a supreme being, but our self-centered disease still tells us that we are responsible for much more than we could possibly control.

When we practice living in harmony with our world, we become wiser about choosing our battles. We learn where we can use our energy to make a difference and where we need to let go. Learning to step away from a conflict once it has started is sometimes harder than not getting into conflicts at all. That doesn't mean that we always agree with anyone or everything, or that we suddenly lose the power to stand up for what's right. On the contrary, we learn when to step forward and when to back away. Some struggles are worth fighting even if we know we cannot win, just as some are not worth fighting even though our victory is sure. This is discernment, and it comes from our experience. We learn to tell the difference between a principle we need to stand for and an opinion that we just won't let go of. We are able to choose for ourselves when to stand up and when to surrender, and as we practice we get better at determining which is right for us.

Learning to accept the things we cannot change and take action where it is appropriate is not just part of recovering from addiction; it is part of growing up. Many of us are like overgrown children, still wanting to have things our way without regard for anything else. Often this means that we go through a painful adolescence in the rooms, whatever our age. Maturity comes to us when we use spiritual principles rather than defects to deal with reality. Incorporating principles into our lives allows us to understand the difference between right and wrong. Many of our most crippling defects become powerful assets when we let go of self-centered fear.

Many times in our addiction we experienced a moment of clarity, when we could see the truth about what we had become, but that awareness in itself did not bring change. Effort is necessary for change to occur. Our lives change because we take action. Some of us say that we are "applying" spiritual principles because it means we're acting in some particular way. Others of us prefer to say we are "practicing" principles because we know we can always get better at it. However we say it, action is what matters.

Our primary action is surrender, and we come back to it every day. There is always room to let go a little more. There is great freedom in understanding that we always have the option to surrender. In the beginning we may be confused and think we need to surrender to our disease; in fact, that's what most of us were doing before we got here! In active addiction, we turned our will over to our disease every day. In recovery we learn to surrender to the process, to the program, and ultimately to a power greater than ourselves. When we give up the battle we place ourselves entirely in the care of a power greater than ourselves. It follows naturally that we commit ourselves to the service of that power, however we understand it.

Surrender means having the open-mindedness to see things in a new way, as well as the willingness to live differently. When we open ourselves to new perspectives we may find more questions where we had hoped to see answers. Each time we can see possibilities that had not occurred to us before, we gain a little more freedom. We are free to change our minds, to change our perspective, and to change our lives. Freedom means that we are no longer living by default. More and more we see how much courage surrender requires.

We see the miracle of recovery in action when an addict we didn't think would make it actually gets the message. We can see new hope in their eyes. The contrast is so sharp that we can't miss it. We can also recognize the miracle when we find words a suffering addict needs to hear even though we didn't think we knew what to say. When we hear ourselves carry a powerful message, we know we are being helped as much as the person we are reaching out to. Finding that we already have the answers we need is like finding a gift on our doorstep. When we are having a hard time, the best thing we can do for ourselves is to accept that gift by helping someone else.

A Spiritual, Not Religious Program

Each of us has our own spiritual path. As we explore our spirituality we find ourselves on a journey of self-discovery. When we live with spiritual awareness, we find harmony with the God of our understanding, with ourselves, and with others. There is no single recipe for spirituality. Each of us finds our own way to live spiritually, and that allows us freedom to make choices about how we live. It also charges us with responsibility.

We cannot pretend that spirituality is not central to the NA program or the NA way of life. But there is room within that for people of all beliefs—including those with no belief at all. Our right to our own spirituality in NA is unconditional, and that also means we must allow that right to others. It's not very complicated, but this is one area of our recovery that we seem to love to complicate. Any single definition of spiritual principles would be too restrictive for us. Our traditions remind us that NA is not a place where any single spiritual path is endorsed.

Finding a spirituality that works for us can be one of the most important challenges that we face in recovery, and yet we are often afraid to talk about it. We may worry that we will feel out of place or that others will be uncomfortable with what we are sharing. When we are carrying the message, we learn to make the boundary clear between our personal spiritual experiences and the message of NA. Finding a balance in which we are open to one another's experience without creating the impression that we are endorsing a particular religion can be a struggle.

While we may pursue a religion or path that uses specific language to refer to spiritual concepts, we ask ourselves how we can express that in a way we can all understand. We use more general language out of respect for all the various perspectives in the fellowship, even though in another setting we might use language more specific to our own particular faith. It can be difficult to find a way to talk about our spirituality and still leave the door open for everyone to have their own path, as well. We use many different words to describe our Higher Power. We do our best to share our deepening spiritual experience in a way that makes it available to everyone in the room.

Most importantly, we find people we trust and respect with whom we feel comfortable sharing one on one. The work doesn't all happen in meetings; we share and explore with our sponsor, in stepwork, or among our trusted friends. We may not ever have to leave NA to find our spirituality, but if our spiritual explorations take place outside the rooms, it is crucial that we understand that NA welcomes us back from every new voyage. Each time, we have new understanding to share and new challenges to work through as a result of our spiritual growth.

One of the most beautiful things about our program is that it works regardless of our different beliefs. NA needs to be a place where we all feel welcomed. Even when we're pretty sure everyone in the room shares the same faith, we still need to make sure that the NA message is clear. We don't limit our application of the traditions to those times when we can see a problem they seem to solve. Keeping our message clear helps us all. "The more I learn to share my spirituality in NA language, the more clearly I can see the connections between my faith and NA," a member explained. When we find ways to share our new insights using our common language of recovery, our ability to carry the NA message strengthens. Our fellowship matures and develops as each of us brings our increasing understanding to the table; we grow from one another's experience when we are willing to share and to listen with an open mind.

Even though it is so central to our recovery, many of us resist talking about spirituality because it comes so close to a conversation about religion. There are many reasons we may be uncomfortable with this. First of all, it's something many of us have learned not to discuss. We know faith is deeply personal. Others of us don't have a way of talking about it without trying to bring other people's faith in line with our own. We already need to change so much that it's important for us to know that our system of faith, whatever it is, will not be threatened by our program. It may be challenged, though, as we begin to practice our spirituality more actively than we had.

We can have philosophical discussions all day long, and never make any progress in our spiritual lives. On the other hand, some of the most spiritual people we know say very little about spirituality. Their quiet example is more powerful than words. The principles we share in the steps, the traditions, the concepts, and the rest of our literature go a long way toward providing us with a common language we can all understand and identify with.

We say over and over that this is a spiritual, not religious program, but that doesn't mean the program can't work for religious people. Some of us come to NA with a foundation in a faith with which we are very comfortable. Others of us find our way to organized religion as a result of the work we do to build a relationship with a Higher Power in the steps. Some of us find alternative spiritual paths, or find that the spirituality we achieve through the program is enough. There is no right or wrong answer on this; there is no progression that brings us naturally toward or away from organized religion. What is important is that we accept that the program is spiritual in nature, that some of what we depend on here is a great mystery, that some of it doesn't make sense. Many of us say that even after years clean, we still don't know how it works; we just know that it works. Allowing the possibility that there will always be something we don't know means that there is always room for something greater than ourselves to work on us and through us.

Some of us have maintained the religious beliefs we grew up with, but in our addiction we compromised ourselves in ways that ran deeply against those beliefs. Many of us had to work so hard to distance ourselves from what our beliefs had been that the way we respond to hearing about them almost feels like an allergy. It can be a long time before we know why that language makes us so uncomfortable. When we start hearing people talk about a Higher Power, it can feel like we're about to be pushed through all those feelings again, and it's natural that this makes us nervous.

We may have negative experiences with religion, or experiences that made our relationship to religion uncomfortable. It can be challenging to face that. Many of us experienced religious efforts to save us from our addiction, and found that faith alone was insufficient to set us free. Or we may have a very well-developed religious faith, and fear that NA is going to ask us to give that up. Whatever our experience, it is critical to our recovery that we find some kind of understanding we can work with. When we are in the process of figuring that out, other people's opinions about what that should be can feel confusing or threatening. It is imperative that we give one another time and space to come to a belief system of our own.

On the other hand, we can be too quick to cut off conversations that some of us need to have in order to reconcile our recovery with our other beliefs. A member confessed, "I have had a struggle with my faith since coming to NA. I still practice the faith I grew up with, and have been very active in it since I got clean. But when I came into the rooms and shared about my spiritual awakenings, I felt shut down. I left for a while to follow that path, but I realize

I need to be here, too—so I find a way to make peace with the gap between them." Without that effort we risk alienating people, or limiting our own understanding of the connections between our spiritual development and our experience in recovery.

Spiritual growth may be a struggle sometimes, but that doesn't mean it's going badly. That struggle is often how we get to a spirituality that works for us. Our beliefs grow as our spirits awaken. When we actually experience our beliefs, they become more vital. For some of us, that means finding a style of prayer that resonates with us; some of us find other ways to make a conscious contact that suits our beliefs. But the key to spiritual growth is that it is growth—which means it changes, and it's going to change us. A member shared, "When I had around ten years clean, I realized I wasn't being honest in my relationship with God because I was pretending I wasn't angry. I realized if I wasn't honest in that relationship, how did any of my other relationships stand a chance?" Each time we recognize an opportunity for spiritual growth, we experience a reawakening of hope.

A Spiritual Journey

Seeking a God of our understanding is a personal experience, but we need to know we are not alone in our search. There is a part of this that is very private, unspeakable in a wonderful way. There are times when we must walk alone with our Higher Power. As we study the traditions, we learn that nothing which affects our personal recovery is an outside issue, and also that our unity must come first. These spiritual principles are not in conflict, but it might take some thought or prayer to reconcile them. When we are living spiritually, awareness and empathy guide us in our recovery and in our sharing. In the Eleventh Step we ask for the power to carry out God's will for us. In that spirit, we may ask for the words we need to talk about our experience without creating separation or disunity around us.

We need to be able to open up about our journey. It doesn't matter so much what names we give the markers along that road. When we learn to share about our feelings and experiences without naming names, we discover the freedom anonymity has to offer us. We may be surprised at how much we have in common with others who seem to be on very different spiritual paths. When we begin to see the things our journeys have in common, we find that our differences really can help us along the way, instead of creating barriers between us.

It can be difficult to express our spiritual experience in words. Because we are talking about things unseen, concrete language usually falls short of what we experience, and the language we have to talk about our spiritual experiences with is often borrowed from other places. It takes practice to make it our own. When we are struggling to find words for our experience, the last thing we need is to be told we are doing it wrong. We listen to one another with an open mind and an open heart, and we share our experience with the understanding that it won't necessarily be shared by everyone else. In the same spirit, we understand that it's hard for other people to share about this, too, and that sometimes we are going to hear things that ask us to be objective and nonjudgmental.

We each find a way to surrender, but that does not mean we all come to believe in God. Many of our members have been clean for years as atheists. For some of us, coming to believe that NA can accommodate our atheism has itself been a leap of faith. We are welcome no matter what we believe. NA has no opinion on how our members define or practice spirituality. Our individual challenge is to find a definition of spirituality that makes sense to us. By listening carefully and with an open mind to a range of members' opinions and experiences, we form our own understanding that we can use in our own recovery. A member shared, "I didn't hear anyone talking about atheism as a legitimate path in recovery, but I accepted that. I did with spirituality what I was learning to do with other aspects of the program: I took what I needed and left the rest behind. Over the years I have accepted that other people's ideas about spirituality, ethics, and God are much different from my own. Part of the strength and beauty of NA is that there is room for all of us. What others call spiritual principles, I call ethical principles."

Whatever they are called, the principles in the steps and traditions lead us away from active addiction, self-centeredness, and fear. When we help someone who is struggling, we break free from our self-obsession. When we give back, we cannot be greedy. We have found no limit to the possibilities of recovery for any member who practices the principles of NA, whether we call these principles spiritual or not.

For some of us, the spiritual is simply the unseen or the intangible. Each of us has complete autonomy and anonymity in whatever concept we find for ourselves. The phrase "as we understood Him" can be a sticking point for many of us. We do not have to understand or accept a Higher Power in order to live spiritually. No one else has the right to judge that or tell us our beliefs are right or wrong. What is important is that we are willing to accept one another's experience with an open mind, and to share our experience without an effort to persuade one another of what is right or true. What keeps one of us clean might not work for someone else. We simply share what works for us.

Being open-minded about our own beliefs as well as those of others frees us from the traps we set in our own minds. We can see our spirituality making a difference in our lives when we do the right thing for the right reason. This is what our Basic Text calls "goodwill." We are able to listen to the voice inside instead of all the chatter around us.

When we get tangled up in our differences and reservations, it's easy to forget why we bother with spirituality in NA. The Basic Text reminds us simply, that "We ease the pain of living through spiritual principles." Addicts feel life so acutely, and it's often this pain that drives us to use even when we know it won't actually make it better. We have been willing to trade even a moment's relief for a lifetime of hardship. Surviving our own lives seems impossible when we get here, but we learn, gradually, to face reality and make friends with the truth. The spiritual principles we practice help to take the edge off that pain, and the more we practice, the more we find that those principles are the keys to freedom. Our lives get easier as we "get clean" in all our affairs. As we practice honesty, integrity, and fidelity, we no longer have to keep track of our stories or cover our tracks. We may be surprised to find that it is actually easier to live this way. We can love our lives, find joy in being alive, and face the world with genuine excitement.

Just as we get fleeting glimpses of God's will for us, we get fleeting glimpses of our own spirituality. Our spiritual condition is always changing. All too often we think we are "unspiritual" because our conscious contact comes and goes, or because we still have unkind thoughts, or because we still act out in ways we wish we didn't, even after many years clean. When we fall short, it doesn't mean that we are not spiritual—it means we are human. After all, if we never fell short, we couldn't practice our Tenth Step! Giving ourselves permission to be human means that we allow ourselves room to keep growing. We are living spiritually long before we know that's what we are doing.

Spirituality is a relationship with reality. As we develop our spiritual lives, we find that reality becomes less frightening and less rigid. We learn to live with our freedom. We come to see that a change in our perspective can totally shift the way we understand our situation. When our lives are based in spirituality, our perceptions and responses are based in an ever-evolving relationship to something greater than ourselves. Self-obsession gives way to humility. We understand that we are not the main character in every play, but that our supporting efforts can make a real difference in the lives of those around us.

As our spirituality develops, we become increasingly grateful for our lives and the people in them. The more good we can see in the world around us, the more grateful we become for the power that brings us to that awareness. When our bodies, minds, and spirits are in harmony, our lives show the difference. We are able to live in balance.

Spirituality Is Practical

As our behavior is more consistently aligned with our beliefs, we come to a new sense of who we are. Even though we have a disease that requires us to be vigilant about our thinking, we can see both good and bad about ourselves. When we take inventory and practice paying attention to our actions and our motives, we sometimes feel like we are defined by our character defects. The most unpleasant things about ourselves are the things that can seem to be the most true. But even though we may see some painful things about ourselves, we know that's not the whole truth about who we are.

We learn that our spirit is not apart from us; it is a part of us. We gain awareness of the exact nature of what is right about us. Our fractured personalities come back together into an integrated whole. Integrity is the state of being fully integrated: Our actions, our thinking, our feelings, our ideals, and our values all match up. It takes a long time for a lot of us to get here, and longer still for us to feel like it's real. More and more, we are able to bring our behavior into alignment with our values and beliefs rather than our feelings and reactions.

When we allow spirituality to be simple, we allow it to be universal. Whatever we believe our Higher Power to be, or even if we don't have one at all, we each have a spirit—the light on the inside that animates us and makes us who we are. "My spirit was the only thing alive in me," said a member. "It was dragging my body around like a reluctant pet. Those times I thought my spirit was dead, it was fine—we just weren't on speaking terms." Newcomers sometimes ask when their spiritual awakening is going to occur.

By the time we ask, it has already started to happen. We may not be able to pinpoint a single moment of spiritual awakening, but we know we are awake now.

As we clear away the clutter that keeps us from the truth, we find that our light shines more and more brightly. It's the beauty we see in the eyes of someone who's really "got it"—a newcomer on that pink cloud, or an oldtimer whose radiance seems to fill a room. We feel it in a meeting, as well. Many of us have walked into a building where several events were happening, and noticed that the room with the NA meeting in it "felt like home."

In the same way, we learn that finding God's will is often just a matter of showing up. When we show up for life with willingness and an open mind, the next right thing tends to present itself. We don't have to look that hard to find it. A sponsor suggested, "Introduce your feet to the floor when you wake up in the morning. Show up to the shower to wash. Show up to your appointments and respect your commitments. When you hit a wall, turn left and find an opening." We learn to listen to our conscience—that still, small voice within that tells us if we're heading in the right direction. The opening is often where we least expect it, leading us to a path, an opportunity, or a miracle we weren't looking for at all.

There is more to creative action than just getting out of the way. Once we start to live, we have infinite choices on where to go with our lives. It begins with showing up for life, but it doesn't end there. Another member shared, "I invite my Higher Power into each moment. Asking for help with my daily routines helps me to love them more. I believe God's will for me is to live in gratitude, even for the little stuff." The ability to accept life on life's terms is an essential part of our spiritual awakening. We can either accept it or stay miserable.

Living spiritually is about recognizing that there is room to grow. A member shared, "It's not a big eureka moment; it's this calm understanding that I am not doing the negative stuff I used to do. I feel myself in alignment with my world." We begin to experience awareness and empathy with others. Our confidence and strength are restored. We see ourselves as part of something greater, and seek to live in harmony with it.

None of this means that we automatically get what we wish for. Our relationship to a power of our understanding is too important to think it can only thrive in good weather. Life gives and takes, and it's not personal. The recognition of our awakening spirit includes being okay with life unfolding exactly as it does, but many of us have moments when we are not okay with what is happening around us. We are in pain, we are frightened, and often we are angry. Sometimes we get confused and think that to live spiritually means that we are happy and get what we want, and that if we're not happy or don't get our way, something is out of balance. It would be nice if that were true, but recovery is not a fairy tale. When we experience loss or disappointment, when we find ourselves faced with news we don't want to hear or situations we'd give anything not to experience, it doesn't mean our spirituality isn't working. In fact, it is at times like these that we can see it most powerfully. Our response to events and our sense of our role in them becomes more proportional and appropriate. We can respond to events without having to under- or overreact. We can live in the present moment.

Walking the Walk

If our relationship to a power greater than ourselves is to be of any use to us, it must be honest. Learning to share our fear, disappointment, and anger takes courage. We pray in different ways. Many of us begin to talk to a Higher Power using formal prayers, and these can be incredibly powerful tools. "I've said the same prayers every day throughout my recovery," one member said. "They worked really well in the beginning. But now, twenty years later, they have a richness and meaning I could not have imagined." In addition, we learn to talk to our Higher Power in less structured ways, sharing our feelings, hopes, fears, and ideas.

It can be important for us to remember to separate the words of a step from what people say about that step. Similarly, our relationship with a Higher Power, as it develops, may not adhere to the model set before us by others, and it may be very different from what we once imagined it to be. In this way, it really is like our relationships with human beings. Intimacy isn't predefined or predictable.

Many of us share that one reservation we have about a Higher Power is that a powerful God would not allow things to happen as they do; what we saw as we endured the hell of addiction could not possibly have been the creation of a loving power. There are a thousand ways out of this corner, and it's not our place to choose one for all of our members. What we find is not that our Higher Power spares us the hardships of life, but that we receive the grace to get through them clean. We can find the lesson in difficulty. We may find that some of the painful situations we once wanted to blame on God are a consequence of our own actions and decisions. Perhaps most importantly, the pain we endure can be transformed into a tool to help others. As we recover and carry the message, we discover that everything we have experienced can be a resource for us to find acceptance, empathy, and the words we need to help someone else find a way up and out of despair. We are powerless over our addiction, but in our surrender we become powerful tools for transformation.

That transformation for each of us begins with surrender. Over and over we find that acceptance helps to free us from pain and suffering. We begin by accepting that we are addicts. From the first time we admit that we are powerless over our addiction and our lives have become unmanageable, we begin to feel relief. And that relief is the very beginning of the gratitude that will guide us throughout our recovery.

Gratitude is not just a mood. It is a course of action, a way of setting ourselves in relation to the world. Sometimes it's a discipline: It can take work to hold ourselves in that attitude, especially when we are used to seeing the world through our filters of entitlement and resentment. Humility and gratitude walk hand in hand. We practice saying what we are grateful for whether or not we feel it. The feeling may not come naturally at first, but when we practice saying "thanks" we start to recognize how much we have to be thankful for. Many of us start with the fact that we're not in withdrawal today. When we start to see how fortunate we really are, our questions don't frighten us as they once did. They may not be answered right away, but we start to see that our questions about the nature of God are much less important than the rewards we get from building the relationship even if we don't understand it or fully believe it.

Spiritual principles seem abstract until we put them into action. Our values are the principles we adopt to guide us. They may change over time, but when we change them for convenience or to please others, we know it. We make that mistake a few times before we learn to recognize it. We may stop acting on our defects, not because it's wrong, but because it just gets too uncomfortable for us. We can't stand the way it makes us feel.

Often we act on spiritual principles before we internalize them simply because we want to save our lives. In the beginning, we learn principles by acting on suggestions. As we integrate spiritual principles into our lives, they become values—that is, we come to value some of them enough that they become part of who we are. When we are learning, we may be very rigid in our practice. As our practices become more integrated into our lives, we find that we can soften a little. "My understanding of honesty was so rigid," said one member, "that I couldn't even be tactful to spare someone's feelings. One day I was caught in a conflict between two sponsees: One called and confessed that he'd done great harm to another, who happened to be in my home at the time. Brutal honesty with either of them would have made the situation much worse. I learned to balance the principle of honesty with the principle of anonymity. Since then I've learned to balance it with kindness and compassion as well."

We use the tools we associate with spirituality from our very early recovery: We practice prayer and meditation, we go to meetings, we take suggestions, we work steps. Once we can identify what our spirituality feels like to us, we recognize that other things in our lives are spiritual.

Making music is an act of prayer for some of us; walking out in nature can be a meditation. "I'm not a religious person at all," said one member, "but I was out in the ocean one day, floating, and I could feel my connection to the water holding me up, and the sky above, and the people onshore, and all of it. That feeling of connection was a powerful thing." When we practice our gratitude by sharing with others, we begin to feel our connection with one another and to something bigger.

Each time we feel that connection—however we attain it—we understand a little more. We see ourselves as part of something greater and seek to live in harmony with it. When we achieve that harmony, the freedom we feel is unmistakable. We are freed from our feelings of alienation and inadequacy, and from the self-centered fear that once seemed to infect all of our thoughts and actions. That freedom comes and goes, but the first time we feel it we are given a new hope that life might not have to hurt so much. Addiction is a painful disease. Our spirituality doesn't kill that pain, but it gives us the ability to move through it, past it, and out into the rest of our lives. We can accept our feelings, feel them, and move on. We begin to trust that the pain we feel at moments in our lives will not consume us. We can start to trust ourselves to feel without fearing that our emotions will destroy us.

Part of learning is making mistakes. We learn as much by missing the mark as we do by finding our target. Inventory is the process of going back over our experience to discover where we were living in harmony with our values and where we were not. If we didn't take personal inventory, pray, and meditate, we wouldn't know whether we were practicing principles in all our affairs. We wouldn't be awake to reality. The steps keep us in tune with the principles, and they keep us in tune with ourselves. As we get better at it, we can identify earlier and earlier the points at which we begin to go astray. Often it's the smallest changes that make the biggest difference in our lives. In the same way that a small change in course greatly alters the destination of ships at sea, small changes in the way we respond to life can free us from old, repetitive patterns and open us to new ways of thinking and acting.

We practice with spiritual principles; we try them out, go to extremes, drop them altogether, and then find which ones have become important to us. As long as we are willing, we continue to change. Our values become clear to us as we act. The principles we once practiced as an exercise, or because it was suggested, become a part of us. Things that are profoundly difficult in the beginning of our recovery become second nature to us. We may not notice this change until we fall away from our new habits for a moment. For example, it can be very hard to start going to meetings again when we have been away for a while. Formerly a habit, meeting attendance once again requires discipline. It gets easier with practice, just like it did the first time.

As we get better at practicing our recovery, we fear ourselves less. We develop new skills and get used to the idea of practicing principles in new areas of our lives, even when we're scared. We come to know that pain can be a catalyst for growth, and not just a threat to our newfound equilibrium. On the other hand, we also learn that pain is not the same as growth; it must spur us to action if we want to find relief from it. We become more willing to take the action that will set us free. As our tolerance for pain starts to diminish, our need for change comes sooner.

Spirituality in Action

Understanding and embracing the steps and traditions is important for all of us. But we must use what we learn, or it is of no value. When we engage in selfless service, we find that all of the principles we have come to love and learn are called upon. It isn't easy to get out of our own way, but that is precisely what frees us from our self-made prisons. Sometimes it is clear that we need to change or we are in trouble; at other times, we are free to stay where we are, but it might mean selling ourselves short. There are many actions we can take when we need to change, but the simplest ones are often the most important. When we give to others, we get out of our own way enough to get a different perspective on our lives. Strangely, the most unselfish things we do are often the most rewarding. Selfless service is service to our Higher Power, our fellow human beings, and ourselves. When we are part of the process, we see a greater power working through us to make a difference in other people's lives. When we see it happen, we have a harder time denying its reality.

We start out in survival mode, and come to live a life beyond our dreams. Even though we have heard it said in meetings for years, it can still be a surprise when our world opens. And sometimes that can be very frightening. There are moments when life opens up before us with so many options that it seems strangely empty. We who have chosen among bad options for years often find that too many choices can make us really uncomfortable. We must come to terms with our own resistance in order to make a commitment to the program. We may be scared to make that leap. There is no way of knowing where it will take us.

We can be afraid to want things too badly because it seems selfish, or because we fear they will be taken from us. Another member shared, "I believed it was unacceptable to fail, and I believed I was a failure. So there really was no out for me. I needed tools to survive my own humanity." Freedom from our old ideas doesn't come easily, and it doesn't all come at once. Thank goodness for that. The truth is, if we went all the way through that process at one time, we might not survive it.

Accepting our freedom is a massive act of spiritual courage. A member shared, "Early in recovery someone told me I could have a life now. It was like I was hearing it for the first time. Life had been passing me by, mostly because I couldn't see myself in it. NA gave me the spirit to be courageous about life again, to just go out and…live!" Our dreams and wishes can be a form of guidance. That "fleeting glimpse" might not be where we are actually going, but it may set the course for our journey.

When we are willing to move toward our dreams, we end up living well beyond them. "I was afraid that if I got what I wanted, there wouldn't be anything left for me to do in recovery," one member confessed. Meeting our goals is not the end of the story. The end of the journey toward a goal is often the beginning of a new phase in our lives. Many of us are used to being driven by crisis or calamity. It can take practice to learn to be motivated by something other than pain. Being willing to step out and act because something feels right to us takes a new kind of trust. "Just as I struggled to list my assets in my first Fourth Step, I struggle to list my goals and the things I enjoy now," one member said. We transform need into desire, and obsession into determination. When we become willing to accept what it really means to set ourselves free, we are in for quite a ride.

After years of recovery, we can look back at the work we have done and be grateful and satisfied—and we can see the terrible gaps in it as well. There is a moment in our lives when we may recognize how much of that work has been in service to the belief that if we do the right things, we will get what we want. When we realize what we have been seeking is not conscious contact but constant comfort, we are appalled. Does this mean that my relationship with my Higher Power is false? Is my recovery a lie? Some spiritual awakenings are also rude awakenings. We see clearly, and what we see may be alarming. When we awaken to the darkness within ourselves, it hurts. "The first time I looked inside and saw the truth about some of the things I had done," said one member, "I thought that was the truth about me. I was terrified. I thought, I've been given the opportunity to see all this grace around me, only to be shown it wasn't for me."

The ability to change our assumptions about the world is one of the most important freedoms we have, because it enables us to see alternatives we couldn't imagine before. We disguised our low self-esteem as lack of interest in the world around us, and saw our lives as a narrow path between bad alternatives. "I saw myself as an obstacle to God's will," said another member. Our relationship to our Higher Power has suffered a lot of damage in our addiction, and it can be one of the hardest to amend.

We know that indifference or intolerance toward spiritual principles is very dangerous for us, but sometimes we develop a different kind of intolerance after we have been clean for a while. We may develop a set of beliefs in recovery and resist anything that seems to threaten them or call them into question. But this is precisely the way that what we know about the truth can be revised. The truth is not what changes; it's what we know about it, how we understand it. As we get closer to the truth we come to understand that it cannot hurt us, even if it is painful in the moment. A member shared, "Letting go of old beliefs was hard because I didn't really know what I believed to begin with." The work we do in the steps can help us figure out what we believe and whether our beliefs still work for us.

"I used to feel embarrassed, strange, and empty when I prayed," another member admitted. "My relationship with my God required that I persevere. I had to keep praying through the times when I didn't feel anything. It took a long time for it to become natural to me." Being willing to keep trying when it feels hard—or when it doesn't feel like anything at all—is an act of faith. We get through these difficult times by having a daily spiritual practice: The habit carries us through until the feelings change. We have faith in the experience of our fellow members that somehow, this practice is going to help.

Willingness to step out and try a relationship with a Higher Power can be powerful, but we may hesitate in the beginning. We put a toe in the water first. We may struggle with prayer and meditation for a long time before we feel something engage. One member shared, "I experimented with different practices for seven years before I found the right grace in the right place. Finding the path for my spirituality was like finding shoes that fit." Another member shared that she was so resistant to prayer that her sponsor resorted to extremes: "Put your Basic Text on one side of the room, sit on the other side, and reach out your hand," said the sponsor. "You have just prayed." However we do it, prayer is an act of reaching out for help and connection. It is an act of humility and honesty, and for some of us it is the first honest or humble action we take.

We can be much more comfortable in an old rut than on a new plateau. We usually don't notice that we're stuck until we have been there for a while, and by then it's hard to break free. We have to be willing to be uncomfortable if we don't want to stay stuck. Trying something new can be its own surrender. It can be very difficult to allow ourselves to experience our freedom. "As an addict I'm a creature of habit," said one member. "The third time I'm in a restaurant, I order the usual." Our comfort with habits makes it easy to stay in a routine. Fear of the disease sometimes makes us afraid to step too far out on a limb, lest we find ourselves in danger. Trying out new perspectives, new beliefs, and new experiences can all be part of living spiritually.

Our certainty can keep us from the humility we so desperately need. Open-mindedness is a cornerstone of our recovery, and that includes being open-minded about our own program. When we stop being teachable, we are in trouble. Too often we create barriers where guideposts are more appropriate. When we build walls instead of pathways, we don't just keep new possibilities out; we lock ourselves into old ways of seeing and thinking about the world. It is easy to get caught in our own trap this way.

When we finally find some relief, we want to hold on to it. As that relief grows into joy and gratitude, it becomes more precious to us. We can be so afraid to lose what we have gained that we hold ourselves back from growth.

We may believe there is only one way for NA to work, and that's the way it has worked for us so far. When a certain practice or way of being has saved our lives, we may refuse to deviate from it. That grit and resolve can save our lives, and it can be really useful when we are carrying the message as well. But with that hard edge comes the risk that we will simply become stubborn and closed-minded, excluding members who don't do it the way we do. When we think we know exactly what the program has to offer, we don't leave room for it to grow or for us to continue to grow within it. Even worse, when the time comes that we need something more, we have convinced ourselves that it won't be available through NA. Our willingness to share our ongoing experience in recovery helps our groups to experience the same growth and renewal that we do as individuals.

We have many beginnings throughout our recovery. Early on we learn that we can begin our day again at any time. As we progress, we learn that we can always begin a new journey in recovery, and we can start over whenever we need to. We don't need to blow up our lives to get a fresh start. We may think we are done when, in fact, we are just getting started. When NA has given us all we have asked for, that's the beginning of a new story for us, a new chapter. The achievement of our goals is a new beginning on our journey, and as the journey continues we will need all of the tools we have been given. Just because we've used them already doesn't mean it's time to turn them in.

Conscious Contact

As we develop more ways to relate to our Higher Power, we find benefits in all of our relationships. For some of us this never comes to involve a Higher Power that we would call God: "I trust the unity in NA," said a member, "that it will reach out to me and be there when I reach out. NA has carried me when I couldn't walk." Learning to pray is a process. The journey is its own reward. "I learned the Serenity Prayer without the first word, because I knew I didn't believe in that. When I was working the Third Step for the first time, I began to pray by saying "thank you." Most of the time now it's not "please" or "thank you" or any kind of dialogue; it just is. I take a deep breath and cherish this quiet moment of being connected."

Prayer helps us to let go of our fear and distrust and to live in faith. We don't have to understand it for it to work. We open the door to a faith deep within that allows us to meet adversity with serenity. "I strive to practice prayer in every moment," said one member. "Of course I fail every day, but it is changing my perspective. I am very aware of the fragility and preciousness of life." Instead of giving so much thought to why things happen, we look for what we can learn. A member shared, "In early recovery my prayers were sporadic acts of desperation and surrender. I learned prayer as a way to practice conscious contact. Now I find if I can remember my Higher Power in the moment, my life becomes a prayer, my wisdom is activated in meditation, and I exist within the will of my Higher Power. I am spiritually free, the farthest from active addiction and the closest to the pure joy of existence in the moment."

Many members believe that our Higher Power communicates with us through the people who come into our lives. One member explained, "Sharing in meetings is my highest form of prayer, because I know my Higher Power is there—I can feel it—and I don't hold back. Often I need another person in front of me so I can pretend I'm talking to them when I talk to God. Sometimes I get answers through them." Active listening is a form of meditation. Some of the most important messages are delivered through some unlikely people. When we listen with an open mind, we can hear the message we need. One of the gifts of empathy is being able to hear one another's truth. We learn to settle inside ourselves. That spiritual peace becomes the root of our emotional stability, and it gives us the courage to take risks. When we can quiet our minds, we can better hear the answers we need. So often we are desperate for answers that are right in front of us.

In some ways, conscious contact with a Higher Power is no different from any other relationship. Meeting a person every day at the same time and place is a good beginning in getting to know someone, but to improve that relationship we have to be willing to share openly. Intimacy grows over time. When we are close to someone through a difficult time, we learn whether we can trust them. The relationships that carry us through hardship are precious to us.

Being present and in the moment, and feeling alive, aware, and connected are feelings we hear about most often when members are sharing about their experiences with prayer and meditation. Most of us don't feel that profound sense of unity in every waking moment, but just knowing that we can feel it sometimes brings a sense of security.

"The fleeting feeling I long for is peace within, based on nothing outside myself. I just have to be willing to put the world down long enough to have a chance at it." Even if we experience that peace for just a moment, we can keep it in our hearts as we move through our lives. A member said: "I was so tired of that committee in my head talking endlessly about how I wasn't good enough and nothing would be alright. So one day in meditation I gave them all musical instruments. You know, they're a pretty good band."

When we notice the word "ritual" embedded in the word "spiritual," we realize how important it is that our spirituality have some kind of regular expression. Practicing principles is just like any other form of exercise: The more regularly and consciously we do it, the better we get at it. "When I don't practice my morning prayer," said one member, "I feel disconnected, like I am running on my own power." Of course, we do not tell anyone how, when, or where to pray. Conscious contact may not involve words at all. But some sort of regular pause for reflection is useful. "I struggle with getting to 100 percent," said a member. "I make good progress toward a goal and then I get scared, back off, and berate myself for not making it all the way there." Regular spiritual practice teaches us the discipline to follow through on other commitments.

The ability to complete a goal comes from the practice of diligence. Developing some autonomy from our negative feelings is one of the rewards of meditation. Our practice helps us to focus and see things through. We remember to put our program first, and to respect our own limits. We strive every day to keep ourselves spiritually balanced. Sometimes we are more successful than others. When we act in love and humility, we are amazed at what we can accomplish. We stop being so afraid of ourselves and find the courage to stand up for what we believe.

Our commitment to Narcotics Anonymous may be the first promise we ever keep. "I always sought freedom from restraints or authority. The way I convinced myself of my freedom was by becoming a nomad. When you are never anywhere for long, you can pretend that your choices don't confine you, that you leave no trace on the world. My emotional luggage was always standing by the door. NA has asked me to do what I have never agreed to do before: to stay." We must come to terms with our own resistance in order to make a commitment to the program. But the unconditional love we learned in the fellowship is one of the most solid things we have experienced. Trusting that gives us the courage to stay through our discomfort.

More and more we find that the principles of the program guide our choices. The ability to choose wisely begins when we are able to be honest with ourselves about our motives and our desires. Sometimes doing nothing is the most spiritual thing we can do. It can keep us from having to make amends later, and it gives us time to seek guidance from our Higher Power. We can have our feelings without being had by them. Laughter and joy can be as spiritual as prayer and service. Some say that enlightenment begins when we lighten up on ourselves.

Creative Action of the Spirit

As we gain more confidence in our spirituality, we become more willing to improvise, not only in our spiritual practice, but in the way we live. We become willing to do the right thing and to let go of fear. We go from simply showing up and reporting for duty each day to a willingness to serve the greater good in the best way we can. We start by following suggestions, and progress to doing the right things for the right reasons. We can stop there—but if we are willing to strive for more, we have the opportunity to exceed our greatest expectations for ourselves. Our experience settles a lot of our ambivalence about spirituality. We can just go ahead and have the relationship with our Higher Power without worrying so much about the things we don't know or understand. Each time an experience reawakens us, we are more aware of the power nudging us to wake up to our lives.

Great or small, our awakenings show in our willingness to practice the principles and carry the message. Service has much to teach us about our spirituality. It's how we show our love and gratitude, but it is also how we learn it. When we act together, we are greater than the sum of our parts, smarter than our decisions, and more powerful than we think we are. The Second Tradition reminds us that a loving God guides our efforts in service, and we can see it clearly when our short-term setbacks or disagreements somehow don't interfere with carrying the message. We see a Higher Power working in NA and come to believe it can work in our lives too. A member shared, "When my home group has put off a decision because some of us aren't sure what to do, we usually make a better decision later. I learned to do this in my personal life: When I take time to pray, I make better decisions."

Some see our service to NA as a training ground: It's where we can learn to practice principles of acceptance and mutual respect. It's not always gentle, but we share a common purpose and a common bond. And because in NA we are all equal and all learning, we are always both the student and the teacher. No matter how long we've been around NA, there always seems to be the opportunity to learn a little more about ourselves when we get involved. "I did some of my early service just to fit in. Over time I have developed a true desire to serve NA. Service makes me feel good about me. I am useful, and I hope and pray each day for new members to join and help carry the message. It takes a long time for NA to grow. To stick with it I have learned patience, hope, acceptance, love, and commitment."

We can do so much in our world. Once we find recovery, our addiction no longer limits us. We are of value in and out of the fellowship. "Today I understand I am an instrument of my Higher Power's will. I have a choice whether I will play in tune, create a new song, or just make noise for its own sake." By adhering to spiritual principles we are able to live, work, and accept situations in the real world, inside and outside NA. When we work the steps in order, we learn to apply them to our daily affairs. If we practice these principles, we never have to use again, and we can continually improve our ability to serve and to cope with what life brings. We admit our powerlessness, ask for help, admit our errors, work on our defects, make amends, and ask for continued guidance. As we apply these principles to our daily thoughts and actions, we enhance the quality of our lives.

We begin to sort ourselves out with the steps as an ongoing part of our lives. Sharing ourselves, whether we are telling our story or reading our inventory, helps us bring order to the chaos. We experience deeper spiritual growth each time we embrace a step. Over and over we surrender, let go, and trust the process; each time another door opens inside us. The gnawing hunger we felt inside is filled as we practice prayer, meditation, and service. As our defects release the chokehold they once had on us, we are freed to live fully. The narrow choices that once defined us give way and we begin to dream, imagine, create, solve problems, or just seek joy in life itself. Our NA program provides a solid foundation. We can use that foundation to achieve anything, as long as it is centered in spiritual principles. We learn to trust the principles of NA to guide us in all our affairs.

It is important to have conviction about what we do. We no longer change who we are to match who happens to be around. Because of this new sense of conviction, we have a clearer path to follow. "Before NA, I was a coward and a follower. My spiritual awakening compels me to stand firm in my beliefs," offered a member. Resentment, fear, and arrogance cut us off from the ability to be spontaneous, creative, and free. We open that channel when we begin to take selfless, loving action. We learn to respect and love people without seeking approval.

We become responsible members of our communities, taking what we learn in the meetings and practicing that in our lives. Service matters in the world. At different times our paths lead us to be of service to others, directly or indirectly. One of the most wonderful feelings we know is that of being a part of humanity. When we practice spiritual principles we experience awareness and empathy with others. Spirituality teaches us to feel human. After so many years of isolation, a feeling of well-being rises within us, assuring us that we are right where we're supposed to be.

We put this way of life into practice with our families, people we work with, and all of our other relationships. We do the best we can each day. Sometimes we improve just a little bit; at other times we make big progress in practicing the principles, or we really fall short. Our progress is not always steady, but we can see it happening over time. We learn to live our principles. We begin to say no when something isn't right for us, even if we might lose someone's approval in the process. We learn to take care of ourselves and our responsibilities, and not to blame others when things don't go our way. We start to see the opportunities for growth that are available to us on our best and worst days.

Hope and freedom from active addiction come to us early and are given freely. This is what some of us call "the pink cloud." We don't have to work for it. But there comes a time when there is no more "just taking." This is a crossroads; many of us stop here and never know what we have missed. We get the real rewards of recovery by giving back and giving forward, out of gratitude for what we have been given, and out of hope for what is to come. Being of loving service is living spiritually. First we take, then we give, then we share. Living fully is a creative expression of love for our Higher Power. To be fully alive, awake, and honest about who we are is a gift to us and from us.

Our spiritual connection leads us forward into a new life of joy, wholeness, and endless learning. We discover within ourselves a passion for living. Our experience is transformed into tools for healing and keys to compassion. We find within ourselves a clarity and beauty we never suspected we had. In whatever way we experience conscious contact, a feeling of acceptance and relief from turmoil seems to come for all of us. The principles of Narcotics Anonymous are the tools we need to deal with whatever life brings. Seeking our Higher Power's will for us brings us ever closer to our own heart's desire: to feel loved, useful, and part of something greater than ourselves.

The spiritual foundation we find in NA gives us the confidence to live and enjoy life, to help others, and to carry the NA message secure in the knowledge that we are guided to exactly where we need to be. We begin to feel connected to the world around us, and our lives have purpose. We find the courage to follow our heart, to listen to the voice within, to create, to commit, to explore, and to live.

We arrive at Narcotics Anonymous hoping for survival. What we find is love, courage, a sense of connection, and a sense of direction. All our lives we had looked for the peace and safety we experience in recovery. As we seek our Higher Power's will for us, we come to an understanding of our purpose. Spiritual awakening is a process. Maybe it is what the whole process is about. We nurture our awakening spirits and know that we are finally free to live in grace, integrity, and dignity.

Our Physical Selves

Each of us has different ways of seeing ourselves. We are physical beings, and we are also spiritual. We are spiritual beings, and we are also emotional. As addicts, we are prone to alienation—the feeling of being apart from—and sometimes we even feel apart from ourselves, as if all these pieces of who we are don't add up to one whole person. When we focus on what is real, we can begin to accept ourselves with all our contradictions. All these pieces of ourselves come together like a kaleidoscope, beautiful and colorful and always changing. We let go of the idea that the pieces need to line up perfectly for us to be okay. We can see amazing harmony in our lives just by being aware of what's happening inside ourselves—physically, emotionally, and spiritually.

We talk a lot about how addiction affects our bodies, but the physical part of recovery is ignored to a surprising degree. We free our minds and spirits, turning them over to a higher power, but our bodies can be another story. Our physical, emotional, and spiritual lives are interwoven: We can think of them separately, but we cannot experience them separately. If we don't deal with the physical part of our recovery, we run the risk of becoming disconnected from our spiritual path.

Taking good care of our bodies can be a challenge. We go back and forth between indulging ourselves in ways that feel selfish or excessive and punishing ourselves or piling on restrictions in an effort to control patterns that feel like symptoms of our addiction. After long struggles with ways and means to drive ourselves back into healthy behavior, we find that what we really need to do is surrender! Often it's when we help a newer member work the steps that we see how they apply to our lives today.

Even though we may have beliefs about what a relationship with our bodies should be like, most of us feel we are not living up to that standard. There are lots of people who want to tell us how we should do it, but taking an honest look at how we relate with our bodies is new and scary. Too often we hold back from the freedom our program has to offer because we are not entirely ready to let go. We are aware of our imperfection, but see it as something we should control, not something we can surrender.

Our sense of humor allows us to squeeze a positive attitude out of a negative self-image. When we are able to laugh at ourselves, we lighten up a little. We do the work, but we also learn to play. We see our defects, but we also see what there is to love about us. Balance in our lives is dynamic, like walking on a tightrope. It only works when we are moving. We are constantly in motion—and so is the way we see ourselves.

It's a Relationship

A relationship with our bodies is just that: a relationship. It can be healthy and rewarding, or abusive and destructive. Mostly, it's somewhere in between. We live and grow, get better and worse, and find that the process is rarely a straight line in one direction. Like any relationship, it requires communication and responsibility: paying attention to our bodies, giving them what they need, caring for them, and seeking help when necessary. For most of us, this does not come naturally. A member shared, "I needed to learn to treat my body like something other than my enemy." Very few of us come to NA with education or experience in what is good for us. Even if we did know better, living through active addiction means we spent long periods of time abusing and neglecting our bodies.

Our relationship to our bodies has been troubled: We spent a lot of time trying to escape them, after all. We pushed the limits, not only through combining drugs, overdosing, or substituting in order to get high, but in other ways as well: staying awake for days and then sleeping almost as long; not eating, or eating in bizarre and unhealthy ways; selling our bodies or engaging in unsafe sex; participating in or exposing ourselves to extreme violence. Our disease craves instant gratification, but learning how to take care of our bodies takes time, and so does healing. We may want results as soon as we start, but mostly they accumulate gradually.

The quality of this relationship varies over time. Sometimes we care for ourselves and sometimes we don't. Sometimes we confuse what we look like with who or how we are, and think that changing our outsides will fix the void we feel inside. Poor self-care can be a sign that we are in trouble, either in terms of our self-esteem or our priorities. When we are not taking care of ourselves physically, chances are we are not taking very good care of ourselves emotionally or spiritually, either. On the other hand, mood changes can be a sign of a physical problem. When we notice a change in how we feel or react, it's usually worth looking a little deeper.

Some issues or life changes bring adjustments to our relationship with our bodies, like quitting smoking, going through pregnancy or menopause, or recovering from an injury. Taking a job that is more demanding than we are used to or working different hours can really affect how we feel and how we take care of ourselves. Emotional changes, too, like beginning or ending a romantic relationship, can change the way we see and relate with our bodies. Whether the changes are ultimately for better or worse is a choice we get to make.

Caring for ourselves leads to other kinds of freedom, including increased energy, freedom of movement, self-esteem, and discipline. We develop the ability to take action in other areas of our lives. If we are resisting a larger change, then we are likely to resist the smaller changes that would make it possible. When we are not taking action on a particular area of our recovery, it's often an indicator that transformation is coming. Breakdown often precedes breakthrough.

Letting Ourselves Go

In the Third Step we make "a decision to turn our will and our lives over to the care of God *as we understood Him*." Most of us make that decision for the first time early in our recovery, but our desire for control expresses itself in many different ways. It is not a decision we make only once. Each time we return to it our resistance lessens, our commitment deepens, and our ability to let go increases. Some suggest that we are in a process of progressive surrenders. We take back control and let it go again, each time finding that we can let go a little more, and that some of what we took back last time we can now let go for good. Next time we look, we find that we are still holding on here and there: "I can turn over this part of my life," we say, "but that other part is my job to handle." Finding the line between personal responsibility and willful control is a challenge. One member shared that for her, "The real surrender is surrendering to the fact that I will be surrendering for the rest of my life." It's different for each of us. In fact, for most of us, the answers change over the course of our recovery.

Feeling at home in our bodies can seem to be beyond our wildest dreams. We feel too fat or too thin, too tall or too short, too old or too young. Some of us feel we were born in the wrong time, place, gender, or culture. We may hardly recognize the person we see in the mirror, or in photographs: "That can't be me!" When something feels wrong inside, we look outside to explain it. Our sense of alienation surfaces in all sorts of ways. We may simply feel uncomfortable in our own skin.

We bring these issues into recovery with us, but it may be a while before we see that they are important. Many of us will share at meetings about having been bone-thin when we got clean; what we talk less about is our response when our bodies start to heal and we begin putting on weight. Some of us find that once the weight starts coming on, it doesn't stop. We might joke that we "put down the spoon and picked up the fork," but it's not always funny. We may feel deep shame or horror at the weight gain. Some of us consider using again to deal with it. We may stay clean but find that compulsive behavior—eating to discomfort, vomiting, fasting, abusing laxatives, experimenting with radical diets—brings its own problems, and its own rush. Obsession with our weight can also lead us back to control games with ourselves: We withhold food, exercise compulsively, and punish ourselves in order to drive ourselves "into shape."

Substitution can be a good tool for keeping us away from that first drug, or for helping us to replace destructive behavior, but it can also create its own problems. Obsessive and compulsive patterns other than using drugs often emerge after we get clean. Many of us find that our relationship to food is complicated. We may never have known how to eat properly, and in our addiction, frankly, other things were more important. We ate irregularly, or we ate junk food, or we didn't eat at all. We got used to being hungry, or throwing up, or eating as much as we could whenever we could.

Our pamphlet *Self-Acceptance* cautions us that "sometimes we slip into the melodrama of wishing we could be what we think we should be." We often act as if that only applies to the parts of us that we can't see. We understand that freedom from our defects of character comes through acceptance of ourselves as we are, and willingness to allow a power greater than ourselves to remove them; but when it comes to what we perceive as our physical imperfection, too often we address the problem through attempts to control or punish ourselves. We invent strict rules and try to live by them. We act as if these obsessions and compulsions were somehow different from those we had already surrendered. It can be difficult to know the difference between behaviors we can change ourselves and those we must surrender. We are on the wrong track when we hold ourselves to unreasonable standards and berate ourselves for failing to meet our own unrealistic expectations. Allowing ourselves to be human does not mean that we live without boundaries or restrictions; it means that we seek sanity in our lives by taking the actions we can and turning the results over to our Higher Power. We let go.

Even though we have so much experience in sharing our struggles with a Higher Power and allowing that power to work in our lives, many of us hold on to the relationship with our bodies as something we must control through willpower. Whether we are learning to eat well, gaining or losing weight, or letting go of smoking or other habits, too often we forget that we have a program that teaches us to be free. Instead we mistakenly say that we have to "get ourselves under control." We may never be free from the disease of addiction, but that doesn't mean we cannot experience freedom.

Fear of change is common among addicts—after all, we are creatures of habit! But sometimes this reaches extremes. We may be paralyzed by our fear. Sometimes what we fear are specific outcomes or consequences. Sometimes we experience a kind of free-floating fear that will attach itself to all sorts of things: We develop phobias, or we avoid risk to a point where it makes our lives very small. Some of us hold ourselves back from pleasure or sensation, either because we are afraid of the future or because we are afraid of the memories that may be unleashed. We fear that letting go might mean releasing our most destructive impulses.

Some of us hide out by not caring for ourselves. We let go of personal grooming or hygiene, gain weight, or simply present ourselves as people we don't care much about. We may want to make ourselves invisible to hide from attention, or to walk away from an old way of being that we don't know how to change. When we admit our fear and look at it honestly, we realize that the actions we take to avoid harm are sometimes more destructive than the consequences we fear. But when we really do let go, we are free to be all that we are, without fear, without guilt, without reservation.

We begin to climb out of the hole we have dug for ourselves when we recognize that our behavior is not working. We practice appreciating small things about ourselves: the unique way we move, the way our eyes glitter when we talk about things that matter to us, the warmth we feel when we know we are connected to our Higher Power. We celebrate the fact that we are unique and have beauty to offer the world. Our uniqueness is our gift; when we forget that, we let the disease back into our lives.

When we fall back into disliking or even hating ourselves, our ability to love suffers. We buy into the old lie that we are not worth it or we're broken. As we let go of the defects of character and other baggage we have been carrying, we begin to uncover the truth of our humanity, our spirituality, and our beauty. Accepting that can be some of the hardest work we will ever do.

Acceptance of ourselves comes as we develop a healthy relationship with reality. We accept what is, and learn to apply the Serenity Prayer, changing what we can and letting go of the rest. We find that we can be happy in our own skin if we are willing to let go—not in the old sense of neglecting ourselves, but allowing ourselves to experience our freedom. We begin to experience our senses. The Basic Text tells us that we are "free to enjoy the simple things in life, like… living in harmony with nature." And it's true! When we see the color in the changing leaves, or feel the wind in our face, we feel the joy of being alive. We find a sweetness in our pleasure that had been gone a long time. Some of us discover that we want to make art; we want to communicate in creative ways. We may value being athletic—to be able to run, or swim, or dance. We lose ourselves in the moment and find, for once, we don't have to think at all. We can just be. When we express the joy we have in living, it comes through in our movement, our work, the shine in our eyes. We have a beauty about us beyond the sum of our features. When we allow that spirit to shine through us, we are beautiful—no matter what we think we look like.

Sex

Asking a room full of addicts how they learned about sex would yield some very strange answers. Most of us struggle in some way with our sexuality. Discovering what is right and wrong for us in this area can be challenging. Each of us comes to terms with sex and our sexuality in our own way. The steps provide us with the tools to come to terms with our past, and to live free of the negative associations some of us have about sex. We start by accepting that there is a lot we don't understand. Being willing to see what has created our views on our own sexuality and the sexuality of others can help us to understand our beliefs.

Many of us are a lot more comfortable with sex than with intimacy. We struggle with issues of self-loathing, contempt for others, and abuse. We may notice that we would rather have unsafe sex than risk a difficult conversation. Having honest, open dialogue with our sponsor brings us to a new level of trust. As we experience intimacy in that relationship, our ability to be intimate with our partners and with others increases as well.

Some of our most deeply held shame derives from the things we did sexually. Our past behaviors may reflect how desperate we were to get and use more, or they may have been the best we could do to find love and connection. Sexual abuse may also be part of our stories. This can be incredibly difficult to talk about. We may believe we are the only ones. On the contrary, it is remarkably common among addicts. Finding the words—and a safe place to say them—can be the difference between being able to live with ourselves and spending our lives on the run from our past. We examine our history in Fourth Steps and begin sorting out who we are from what happened to us or what we did. Healing takes time, but it does happen. We must be patient with ourselves. Gradually, we come to experience freedom from some of our deepest wounds. As we begin to clear up some of the confusion and contradiction in our lives, we can move forward with less of the baggage we brought in with us.

We struggle with relationships. Experienced members suggest that we give ourselves a break for the first year, stay out of relationships, and put our recovery first, but few of us heed this wise advice. We come into recovery lonely, horny, and insecure. We are emotionally raw, and our judgment is still pretty impaired. We run headlong into relationships only to discover how challenging they are. Two sick people rarely make a well couple. We mistake novelty for love and find ourselves deep in commitment almost before we know each other, or fear commitment so much that we don't give our partner a chance. We open the door for relapse when we get caught in loops of obsession and compulsion. We try, and sometimes we make mistakes. Each mistake carries a gift and a hazard: We can learn from our mistakes and use them, or let our guilt and remorse drive us into a corner or out of the program. The more practice we get at using the steps and other tools of recovery, the more we are able to use our mistakes to propel us forward.

We define ourselves partly through our sexuality. For some, that definition is a major portion of our identity. Sometimes we seem to wield it like a weapon to justify our feeling different. We can be much more aware of the people who are not open to us than those who are. In the rooms of NA we are welcomed regardless of our sexuality. We find people who love us and with whom we feel comfortable no matter what our sexuality or our beliefs about sexuality.

Although some of us arrived in the fellowship secure in our sexual identity, others of us struggled with confusion or distortions about our gender or orientation. We may have engaged in behaviors that conflicted with our beliefs in order to continue using or to gain acceptance from others.

Or we chased sex the same way we chased drugs, feeling just as powerless and out of control. Some of us followed those drives into relationship after relationship without ever really feeling fulfilled. Many of us confused sexual connections with intimacy, and became so divorced from our feelings and desire for emotional connection that we would settle for physical interaction. This can follow us well into our recovery and may point to an ongoing struggle with opening up to emotional intimacy. For those of us who used sex as a way to move through the world, it may take quite some time to figure out the difference between being sexual and being intimate. Working through these issues takes time, trust in our sponsors and close friends, willingness to challenge our assumptions, faith in the process, and ultimately self-acceptance.

The next chapter will address our relationships in more detail. What we will say here is that part of learning how to live in our bodies is learning how to acknowledge the reality of our sexuality. We want to learn to express our sexuality in healthy, and fulfilling ways—something that was unimaginable in our active addiction.

Sex is different when we're clean. When we are neither numbed out nor artificially stimulated, we can be present to our own experience and to our partner in a very different way. Sometimes this can be frightening; sometimes it can be addictively exciting. Finding pleasure in our sexuality without thinking of it as a means of exchange or power can be a great freedom; for some of us, this takes longer than it does for others. We can enjoy ourselves and each other fully, in the moment, and learn what it really is to connect. We can be intimate. We can open up and be real. We don't have to use each other as a drug; when we treat each other as human beings, we find our own dignity.

Thrill-Seeking and Adventure

Long after the obsession to use is lifted, many of us still seek a "rush" in other ways. The drive for excitement leads us to live full and exciting lives, rich with adventure. We are unafraid to take risks and pursue the opportunity to do the things we always wished we could. Sometimes, though, it seems like we just get strung out on our own adrenalin. Whether it's gambling, sex, or creating drama in our lives, we can ramp up so fast that it's hard to scale back down. We may distract ourselves with risky behavior when we are trying to fill a void or block a feeling. It is up to each of us to find a balance between chasing a destructive rush and really living our lives to the fullest.

Surprising numbers of us are fond of extreme sports. A member who spends his weekends scaling glaciers said: "In those moments when I really am on the edge of life and death, when I'm not sure how I'm going to find my next foothold, then I feel present to the moment. I'm not thinking about the bills or the wife or the job, just how good it is to be alive and how I'm going to stay that way." Some of us take on competitive sports or bodybuilding and get really excited about what we are doing. We find a passion and commitment for these activities that seemed lost to our addiction. We have the freedom to try new things and take new risks.

Many of us are partial to motorcycles, and a similar impulse may lead us to ride. We like the sense of freedom, as well as the power and the risk. Some of us drive our cars very fast, and share that the excitement is not just going fast but knowing we're getting away with something. We may think this doesn't apply to us, until our sponsor suggests that we try obeying all traffic laws for a week—just as an experiment. While some of us find acceptable ways to chase the rush throughout our recovery, others find the need settles down after a while—or the wreckage we create just gets to be too much.

Sometimes, without an outlet for our energy, we just sit in our own anxiety. It can be surprising to learn that anxiety comes from the same source as our enthusiasm; it can be useful energy if we channel it, or it can be incredibly destructive. The same power that fuels our destructive impulses can fuel our excitement, creativity, and ambition. It can drive us to adventure or chaos. Like so much of what we uncover about ourselves, it can be an asset or a defect, depending on how we use it.

"When I found myself in self-centered fear," said one member, "I would take risks that could ultimately cause me to lose everything. I was living on the edge clean so I could feel something other than the abyss of not using. I filled the void with things like gambling, shopping, anything that made me feel powerful when I am powerless. Now that I can see myself more clearly, I realize that I have to be more aggressive with treating my disease, taking its deadly nature into account."

At some moments, it may feel like we are holding on to our recovery with both hands. There are times when we just bulldoze through an obsession to use or act out in some other way. There are times when fear of our disease leads us to shut down, resist change, or fear novelty because anything that takes us out of our routine might put us at risk. But recovery doesn't always have to be about ducking: When we know our lives are in the care of a loving power greater than ourselves, we are able to let go. Some of us express this very literally, going skydiving or bungee-jumping as a way to really step out. For most of us, though, letting go is a little less dramatic. We start to experience life as an adventure, and apply that willingness to try in other areas of our lives.

Wellness and Health

Life is an adventure, and we are able to go further and experience more than we had ever dreamed. We are able to live beyond the barriers we set for ourselves when we surrender to the real limits before us. Another door opens every time one closes: With self-acceptance comes a willingness to creatively explore new directions. Many of us have regrets about time or abilities lost, but when we really start to explore with an open mind, we find that we have options we may never have considered.

We have had a difficult relationship with the word "should." We have spent much of our lives rebelling against the things others expected of us, but when we get clean we find we have long lists of things we think we "should" be doing. We can be so full of "should" that no matter what we are doing, it feels wrong. Our expectations of ourselves can be so overwhelming that they cripple us. Part of developing new habits we can sustain is finding better reasons to do them than that we "should." Behavior that brings its own rewards is much likelier to become part of our lives than the things we take on because we imagine it's what we should do. We may have to persist a while before we find that reward, however. Whether it's the peace we find in the course of exercising or the gratification of seeing ourselves develop or improve a skill, we are pleased to find that we can keep a commitment to ourselves.

For some of us, exercising is something we do—or think we should do—to take care of our health. But for others, it's deeper than that. "When I'm running," said one member, "I get a sense of prayer. My mind becomes clear." Finding a spiritual connection in exercise is easier for some of us than meditating while sitting still. Exercise can be easier to keep up when it is part of our spiritual practice than when it's simply a matter of doing what we think we are supposed to do.

Some of us see self-care as an ongoing part of the amends process. We start by not engaging in self-abuse and gradually learn to treat our body, mind, and spirit with honor and respect. When we care for our own well-being as we would an honored friend, we begin to feel differently about who we are and who we can become. We shift from "I should" or "I have to" to "I get to" and find that caring for ourselves isn't a chore; it's a privilege. When we treat ourselves with compassion, we learn to value ourselves. Exercising regularly can be a way to act on our new self-respect, and to build a different relationship with our bodies. We can let go of some of the emotional turmoil about what we look like or think we look like, and begin to love ourselves as we are. We are able to walk with dignity and treat others with respect. We start to view ourselves with a sense of unity: We let go of the idea that "my body" is separate from "my spirit" or "myself."

We feel refreshed and renewed physically, and realize that we are able to push ourselves beyond what we imagined our limits to be. Setting physical goals for ourselves and achieving them can have immense rewards. As we find freedom from our disease through practicing the principles of the program, we learn that discipline is actually a part of that freedom: We have the ability to pursue our dreams, and we get there one goal at a time.

We may resist meeting goals or getting "too healthy." We hold ourselves back from all we can be, either because we feel we don't deserve it or because we are afraid of the change it will bring. Sometimes praying for willingness can begin the process of change. An act as simple as preparing a proper meal for ourselves can be the first link in a new chain; as we incorporate healthy patterns in our lives we begin to feel refreshed, renewed, and willing to set new goals for ourselves.

It can take a long time to let go of the belief that somehow the ordinary rules of life don't apply to us, from the speed limit to the laws of physics. Having courted death for so long, some of us seem to think we are immune to it. Even though we know better, the powerful sense of entitlement that enabled us to do what was required to maintain a habit doesn't go away immediately, and many of us struggle with the feeling that being clean is such a triumph that the world ought to celebrate—and give us what we want.

For some of us, that false sense of entitlement runs so deep that taking care of ourselves does not occur to us as our responsibility; that had been the task of our partners, medical professionals, or the warden. Our readings suggest that "through our inability to accept personal responsibilities we were actually creating our own problems." It benefits us to sit with our sponsors and consider what our personal responsibility really is: What are we responsible for, and what are we not? When we look at it, we may find that we feel more responsible for others than we do for ourselves. Learning to care for ourselves is part of taking personal responsibility, and it can be surprisingly difficult.

One of our oldtimers used to share that "there is nothing sadder than an addict with a high tolerance for pain," and the truth is many of us struggle with that. Some of us have endured great physical hardship or abuse; many of us have borne terrible emotional suffering. It makes sense that we take pride in being tough. Strength seems like its own reward, and it's certainly a survival skill we're not too keen on letting go. For a lot of us, that strength is a part of our identity, both in terms of how we see ourselves and how we want to show ourselves to the world. What could be wrong, after all, with being able to tolerate so much?

The answer is in the question. When we see a using addict with a high tolerance for pain going on to the bitter end, we can see how needless that suffering is. But in our own lives we may not notice when we are doing the same thing. As we work the steps, we come to see that we tolerate more than we need to, and probably more than is healthy for us. One member shared, "I no longer live at the animal level in obvious ways, but when I ignore persistent pain in my body and just wish it would go away, that's still a form of needless suffering." Learning that the rules really do apply to us means that when something is wrong, we stop and take a look at it.

Being a good steward of our bodies means accepting that they need care and maintenance. As we recover, many of us find that we have a new importance in the lives of our families. We develop deep friendships; we become useful in our work and our communities. Where once we may have been a burden to others, we now find that we are important to many people. We matter! Not taking care of ourselves, living self-destructively in recovery, we find the old lie "I'm only hurting myself" still falls flat. For the people who care about us, failing to care for ourselves is frustrating at best. Too often, it leads to the result that once again they are taking care of us. Taking care of ourselves is an act of amends not only to ourselves, but to the people who love us, and to our Higher Power. It's a way of showing gratitude for being alive.

Illness

Many of us suffer from diseases other than addiction. Some may be a direct consequence of our addiction or things that happened while we were using. Others may have nothing to do with the disease of addiction but certainly impact our recovery. Sometimes it seems like they take over our entire lives. Learning to use the tools we gain in NA to cope with our other challenges is part of living life on life's terms.

When we suffer, or see someone else suffering, we want to make sense of it—so we look for an explanation. It's a good impulse that can go sideways: We want an explanation, but we end up placing blame or passing judgment. Often in the moments when we most need comfort and care, we are angry—at ourselves, at our Higher Power, at anyone in between. We push away what we need the most. Fantasies about what is or is not "fair" keep us in resentment and self-pity. Sometimes when we are trying to support our friends by helping them find an explanation, it can feel like we are just heaping on more blame. We can shift perspective slightly and look for the lesson rather than the explanation. It may be that what we really need to do is set all the questions aside and just get through the day.

When something is going on with our health, we have a choice to accept what is happening and deal with it or pretend it is not there. A great deal of the time we choose to ignore what we know, either because we are afraid or because we don't want to hassle with it. For some of us, the fear of undergoing medical treatment is understandable, especially if that brings with it the possibility of having to take medication. Weighing risks and benefits is not easy. Finding a doctor we trust makes the process easier. We carefully consider the possibility that leaving a problem untreated may create more problems than before. Turning something over is not the same as ignoring it. When we take action and leave the results to a power greater than ourselves, we are turning it over. However, when we don't take responsibility for our part, but wait for a magical answer, we are not working the Third Step; we are being irresponsible. Faith is not the same as wishing.

There is a difference between denial and refusal: When we are in denial we don't know it. The evidence may be glaringly obvious, but we do not see it. Once we can say, "I'm in denial," it is no longer quite true. At that point we are making a choice to accept what is real, or to turn away from it and pretend. When we refuse to admit the truth, we are in danger. Rebellion can be deadly for us. "Acting as if" is a tool we can use for better or for worse.

The fear that keeps us from moving forward can stem from many causes. Other people's opinions of us may still seem important enough to risk our lives for: The stigma of disease, whether from society at large, our loved ones, or even our friends in NA, keeps many of us from seeking testing or treatment. Our own judgment and fear can be surprising as well. In early recovery, we learn about projection: What really bothers us about someone else is likely true for us too. So it is with this fear: What we imagine others to be saying about us is often what we are thinking ourselves. We may need to drive ourselves to take action long before we are done working through our feelings about it.

We may be surprised that a dental problem, for example, could return us to the Sixth and Seventh Steps. But when we recognize that our fear is preventing us from taking care of ourselves, we can see the work we have to do. Sometimes it can help us to look at this action as part of the amends process; we are dealing with the wreckage of our past. A member shared, "I spent a fair portion of my second year in recovery getting my teeth fixed, and I noticed many others doing the same thing. It was a huge self-esteem thing, and an amends to my body." It may help to see it as part of a Tenth Step, addressing what is wrong in the present moment. Some of us have felt that we created our health problems as a result of our addiction, and that this is simply our lot. The Basic Text tells us that although we are not responsible for our addiction, we are responsible for our recovery; it may help us to consider that this applies to our bodies as well as our spirits.

We may also be genuinely afraid of being sick. Whether it's the particular diagnosis we're considering or the general idea of having something "wrong with us," this may be a kind of powerlessness we don't feel at all ready to accept. We may fear that our health issues will create new uncertainty in our finances, our careers, or our families; or that medication will put our recovery in jeopardy. Our fear of something so far out of our control may be surprising in people who have taken so many really insane risks, but feelings don't always make sense. Fear gives us a chance to act with courage. When we stand up, face what's wrong, and deal with it to the best of our ability, we may not feel very brave at all; but these are the moments at which we serve as the most powerful testimony to what is possible in NA. We are demonstrating strength of character.

When we use the tools available to us—calling our sponsor and seeking the experience, strength, and hope of others, allowing our support group to support us, and turning to *In Times of Illness* and other NA literature—we are able to make decisions we can be comfortable with, and take action to do the next right thing. These can be the moments that define our recovery.

We may start trying to make deals with God, promising all sorts of things if this will just please go away. This type of bargaining is not uncommon, but it is dangerous, and frequently unhelpful. When we start trading on promises and expectations in our prayers, we are setting ourselves up for spiritual crisis. A Higher Power is not a vending machine. When we accept life on life's terms, we come to understand that the terms are not negotiable. Miracles happen to us and around us all the time. The very fact that we are alive and clean to face this challenge is a miracle, and there are always more unfolding if we look for them.

Gratitude may be most needed when it is hardest to find. Looking for the reasons we have to be grateful in a moment of crisis can make all the difference. But daring or demanding miracles doesn't seem to work very well. We take action, and turn the results over.

Surrender in times of illness can mean a lot of different things. We surrender to the process; we surrender to the fact of mortality and to the possibility of survival. Surrender in this sense does not mean giving up. One member in the midst of a long illness said, "It was pretty easy for me to surrender to the possibility of dying. It was a different kind of surrender for me to become willing to fight for my life."

There is no model of the recovering addict, no one right way to do things. Some of us, taking an honest look at ourselves and our lives, really don't want to live that long. It may sound odd, but it's true: Longevity is not a universal goal or necessarily a universal good. Some of us make choices knowing they will shorten our lives. We may choose to smoke; we may choose to eat in a way we know is harmful; we may make a decision to stop or refuse treatment for an illness. A member whose parents had a difficult old age said, "I'm not going to do that to my daughter. I have a life I love, but that doesn't mean I want to play the hand to the end." We may be surprised at some of the decisions we make, or the strength of our feelings about them. These decisions are deeply personal and we make them in accordance with our values. We want to be certain that we are acting on our beliefs, not opening a reservation that could lead us back to using. Each of us finds a balance we can live with between taking perfect care of ourselves and neglecting ourselves destructively. Whatever choices we make, what matters is that we know we are making them—that we understand we have a choice, and we consider it honestly and openly.

We are always on a continuum between health and illness, between action and wishing, between living in accordance with our beliefs and betraying ourselves and our values. We come back to the tools of the program again and again to fine-tune that balance, and to find a way to bring ourselves back to a life we are comfortable with. Our process of inventory, amends, and surrender is an unending source of improvement for us. We find our values and learn what it means to live by them. Over time we can let go of our expectations for what we thought life was supposed to be, or what we think others expect of us, and live according to the values we find within ourselves. As we learn what is true for us, we find that we are less compelled either to be perfect or to destroy ourselves. We are free to live lives according to our own choosing and design.

Disability

"Just for today," says our reading, "I will try to get a better perspective on my life." Even though most of us addicts resist change, we know that it is beneficial for us to change our perception by changing our perspective. Nothing changes our perspective quite like the experience of disability. Chances are, if we live a full life, we will at some point experience disability—whether for a relatively short time or in a way that changes our lives permanently. In either case, the lessons that we learn through the experience can enrich our lives and broaden our understanding, even if some of our choices are narrowed.

We know that our recovery must come first, but when we are dealing with disability, more than that is necessary to get through each day. Some of us enter recovery with a permanent disability already a part of our lives. Our experience has shown that any addict can recover, and the additional challenges that a disability presents are not barriers to our way of life. As one member shared, "I know there will never be any sort of recovery from my blindness, as this program has given me from my addiction; but my perception of my disability can improve, and from that my spirit. Just like a sighted member, it all boils down to self-acceptance. I simply have something more to accept."

"Argue for your limitations," the saying goes, "and they are yours forever." We may be so painfully aware of our limitations that we can hardly imagine ourselves without them. We mourn for the abilities we have lost, and we fear what is to come. Many of us struggle with having to ask for help. Frustration at little things—uneven pavement, the buttons on a shirt, things others might take completely for granted—can be overwhelming and discouraging. We may be surprised at the amount of time and thought involved in doing the simplest things.

To try to talk about gratitude at a time like this seems preposterous and infuriating. We may think, "You just don't get it; you have no idea what this is like." Self-pity is no less dangerous when we feel justified than when we know we are out of line; either way, it can kill us. If we have been around a while, we know that gratitude is almost always the shortest road to relief. Some of us find gratitude in the knowledge that it could be worse, and find relief in helping out—or simply being aware of—those who are struggling with even greater challenges. For some of us this is cold comfort, but we find gratitude when we pay attention to the things we do have—starting with people who care about us, and a relationship with a loving Higher Power. A gratitude list can be a vital tool at times like this. One oldtimer used to growl, "If you can't find anything to be grateful for, start with the fact that you're not on fire and work your way up from there!"

Learning to reach out to members with additional needs can be a process, as well. Asking how we can help, rather than assuming what someone needs, is an act of empathy. We learn that simple assistance, offered reliably and without much fuss, can be a powerful form of love and acceptance. Our customs or policies may need to be adapted in order to allow a member to experience the joy of service, regardless of physical ability.

Disability doesn't disqualify us from service; on the contrary, it may make us more aware of the needs of our members and the obstacles to recovery for addicts still suffering. There are ways for everyone to give back in NA, even if we have to be a little creative about how we can best serve. We can be powerful examples of commitment and willingness when we look past our own obstacles to help others. We may become very conscious of issues of access, even if they only affect us for a short while. We notice whether a meeting list tells us which meetings we can get into with a wheelchair, for example. We start to look more carefully at what makes a meeting feel safe and welcoming. The meeting whose doorway is level but whose bathroom is upstairs is as inaccessible as a meeting on the moon for some of us. When we bring our experience and our awareness with us into service in our local NA community, we help to ensure that the message is available to all addicts, regardless of mobility or other access issues; in this way, our challenge may help the fellowship as a whole to carry the message more effectively.

In times of need, we almost always find that NA members are here for us, but it may not be the people we expected, or the people we wished for. It is surprising to see who is ready to walk through a difficult time with us, and who is not. Anonymity inside the fellowship means that we are all equal. Each of us has abilities that are valuable and limitations that are regrettable, and together we can do what we cannot do alone. We allow ourselves to be open to the people who are ready to walk with us, rather than focusing on our disappointment in those who aren't there. Although we might wish that people would act according to our expectations, we don't want to miss the little miracles of seeing those we never thought had it in them stepping up to the plate and really helping out.

The lessons we learn in NA about sharing and caring, asking for help, and offering what we have to give are powerful tools we can use outside the fellowship as well. We may feel a new bond with other people who struggle with physical challenges and find that our shared experience brings us closer. We may find relief in being with others inside or outside the fellowship who are struggling with the same kinds of issues and finding ways to adapt.

Our pride can be a bigger handicap than the physical challenge we are confronting. Pride tells us that we want to look good, and this puts a serious crimp in our style. Embarrassment, shame, or unwillingness "to be seen this way" may keep us from doing what we can, or really living and enjoying our lives as they are. Our physical disability can become an alibi for isolation, withdrawal, and fear, if we let it.

Gradually, we find that the disability that has forced a change in our habits also changes the angle from which we see the world. We notice details we missed before; we connect with people we hadn't seen before. As the rhythm of our life changes, so does the music. We learn to respect rather than indulge our limitations, and to build our skills and assets in new areas. We learn time and again that some of our best gifts come in the worst wrapping paper. Being open to the lessons in every experience helps us to get through even the hardest times; knowing that we don't have to do it alone sure makes it easier.

Emotional and Spiritual Crisis

We talk a lot in the rooms and in our literature about the insanity of our addiction, and while it is quite clear that our thinking is deeply distorted by our disease, this is distinct from other forms of what professionals call mental illness. Our booklet, *In Times of Illness*, can be a very helpful resource for those of us struggling with mental illness in recovery.

Mental illness is real, and can be very serious. It is vital that we understand that while the illness itself is an outside issue that needs treatment, our struggles with our mental illnesses and the way they impact our recovery are very much "inside issues." We need to make this distinction to ensure that we don't fail to seek additional help either because of stigma in the rooms or confusion about the relationship between mental illness and recovery. But it is also essential that we understand that we can feel pretty depressed, anxious, or out of control without having a mental illness.

Sometimes what we experience is a consequence of a physical condition: When we're detoxing, for example, things can get pretty intense. Most of us in early recovery find that we lack a "volume knob" for our emotions: Our moods swing wildly, our lives seem very dramatic, and we can be startlingly impulsive. As long as we are not a danger to ourselves or others, many of us find that we can wait this out—things settle down as we get used to our new lives, and as our bodies get used to being clean. Sometimes we look insane, but we just need more time. "Emotional detox" can take a lot longer than physical detox, and there are days when it's really hard. The time we sit in meetings may be the only time our racing thoughts slow down at all. Having people around us who have been through what we are going through and come out the other side is very reassuring: We may not be convinced this will pass, but our sponsor's confidence can give us hope.

Other physical changes put us through emotional challenges as well. Some physical illnesses or head injuries have emotional or cognitive components, and those of us who struggle with other physical diseases may find our thinking is sometimes profoundly impacted by them. When we or our loved ones notice a sudden change in our behavior, it is worth considering whether there may be physical forces at work.

But there is not always a physical or organic cause behind our disturbance. We go through intense emotional changes in recovery, and they can be frightening. Too often we mistake spiritual crisis for mental illness. Grief, depression, or panic may come over us in a wave; memories come up from the past and seem to swallow our present; and all of this can be part of the process we go through on our way to freedom. What we really want is a cure for our feelings.

The pain of spiritual growth can feel like depression. A "dark night of the soul" can be frightening and lonely. But what is happening on the inside is often the process that will bring us into the light. Sometimes there's just bad weather in our heads and we simply need to wait it out. Hanging on, suiting up, showing up, and sharing openly with our sponsor and other members we trust is sometimes all we can do while it passes. We talk about "the process" and are told to trust in it, but we don't always know what "the process" is. We may be very confused by where it seems to be taking us. If we focus on putting our faith into action, we can come through difficulty with new understanding and awareness.

This kind of crisis can be frightening in its intensity, and sometimes it seems we can only distinguish it from another kind of struggle in retrospect. Intense as it is, it is temporary, and relieved by breakthrough or by an obstinate willfulness to hang on until the crisis passes. "We undergo a vital spiritual experience and are changed," says the Basic Text. We can be restored to sanity and live happy and productive lives. But it may not be safe or sensible to wait to find out what kind of crisis we're having before we seek help. We may need new tools to continue to build our house; it doesn't mean we are abandoning the work we have done or betraying our commitment if we sometimes go looking for them elsewhere.

Some of our more experienced members have shared that moments of deepest insanity occur when our insides don't match our outsides—when we are doing things that go against our beliefs, when we are in one way or another living a lie, or when we are in denial of what's really happening around us. The disconnect between what we want, what we believe, and what we are doing is enough to make anyone feel insane—and can be a powerful force for relapse. Coming back to living in integrity begins with sharing honestly with one person. It may be a long road back, but the alternative can be so painful that we may not survive it clean. When we tell our sponsor or trusted friend what's really going on, we can begin to feel a little hope again.

Aging

Life passages everyone has to deal with are changed for us because of our disease. They may be magnified by our obsession and self-centeredness, or we may simply be more dramatic than our nonaddict friends and neighbors. But we also have physical challenges to deal with that are a consequence of our addiction—the high cost of low living, some have called it. Many of us have other diseases as a result of what we have been through, and we may struggle to get through the shame and guilt we feel before we are willing or able to get treatment. Some of us experienced trauma—violence or abuse that has consequences long after the bruises have healed. "Getting in touch with my body has been a very slow process," said one member. "Any new information from my body just felt like panic." We have been in accidents, violent relationships, fights, war, prison—all of these situations had physical and emotional consequences that manifest in different ways over time.

For some of us, there is the simple, strange experience of having lost time: When we get clean we may feel like we are waking up from a long nap. "I look in the mirror and there's an old woman looking back at me," said one member, "and every time it's a shock. It seems to me that the last time I looked I was just starting out. I still feel like a kid, but I look like someone's grandmother."

The likelihood that we would die is less alarming for some of us than the possibility we might get old. Staying clean a long time is one thing; allowing ourselves to age is quite another. And some of us, as we see it happening, grieve. We may grieve for a long while over the time and opportunities lost to our addiction. We may experience that sense of loss after we have been clean for many years—when, for example, we become a grandparent and realize how much of our children's lives we missed. We may not have noticed that time has passed at all, until someone points out to us that our friends or the people we date are a generation younger than we are.

Normal social pressures to look young or stay pretty are magnified for us by our self-centeredness, but also by the sense of lost time, the feeling that our looks are something we trade on, and that old addict fantasy of dying young and glamorously. When we realize we are too old to die young, and that we might just be around to live a long and full life, some of us have mixed feelings. There is gratitude but also a sense of despair: "I hadn't prepared for this," we think. Some of us seek to preserve our youth as best we can, working hard to dress and care for ourselves so we look and feel younger. Some of us realize that we have planning to do, and take action to ensure the future for ourselves or our children. Finding the balance between vanity and self-respect, between self-loathing and self-acceptance, is a struggle for many of us. When we finally surrender, we find that aging too is a journey, and we can actually enjoy the adventure. We are not just growing old; we're growing up!

A member shared, "There really isn't too much to this aging thing except self-acceptance, and what your body does." Like so many things in recovery, it sounds so simple from the other side, but getting there can be a long walk. It might be impossible to separate the changes that come with graceful aging from the changes that come from working steps; together, though, the combination is remarkable. As time has passed and our fellowship has aged, we have started noticing some of our oldtimers getting more and more beautiful. There is something about spirituality that radiates through our outer being, a sort of agelessness that appears as elegance and dignity. Although we may fear growing older, many of us find that we can embrace and love what we have become—aches and pains and all. "As I have aged and have more trouble getting out of the chair without leaning on the table," said another, "I am more secure about who I am. I find myself more attractive than when I was a hot tomato!"

Death, Dying, and Living with Grief

Addicts die. We talk about it in our literature, we remind ourselves at every meeting that the ends of our disease are "jails, institutions, and death," but when one of us dies we generally respond the way anyone else would: with shock, surprise, and anguish. When we lose a member to the disease, we may go back through the same reservations we experienced in early recovery that the program doesn't really work. Many of us experience other reservations at this point as well—the feeling that it doesn't pay to care so much about people, the sense that loving addicts only results in loss and hurt. For some of us, staying in the fellowship after a painful loss can be very difficult. It's not unusual to feel that others are grieving wrong, that people aren't responding appropriately. When we are hurt and angry it is easy to lash out, harder to feel compassion and connection. But experience has taught us that these are the things that make it easier to get through difficult times clean—even grief.

Of course, losing addicts to the disease of addiction isn't the only way we experience death in recovery. Addicts die clean, too. We lose members of our family, we lose friends; sometimes it seems like the more connected we are, the more opportunities there are to experience loss. And in a sense, it's true: We love more, we care more, we share more than we ever have, and perhaps more than people who are not members of a fellowship like ours. One of the rewards of recovery is that our lives are so rich and full of people we care about, but we do lose some of them, and it's hard. Sometimes what we feel is the guilt of having survived: We may never understand why some of us live long, full lives and some of us are gone so early. For many of us, the answers we find in the steps carry us through the very real moments of doubt. But they are very particular, and can be different for each of us. The grief process forces us to make peace with unanswered questions, and in that way it is a gift.

Some of us find that a death we experience in recovery triggers feelings left over from earlier losses that we never really had the chance to grieve. We have learned through working the steps that emotions we don't feel in the moment often wait and catch up with us later; the experience of walking through a loss in the present can bring back long-forgotten losses from our past. We have been surprised by the force of our emotion at the loss of a friend, or even a pet. We may have thought we could get through the feelings relatively easily and find that we are floored by the experience. Others of us find that there is still some distance between ourselves and the world, or that our reactions are not so immediate. Sometimes our feelings aren't as deep as we think they should be; we think we are supposed to be having a particular experience, and we are feeling something very different. Giving ourselves permission to have our feelings and not judge them is a powerful gift we can give ourselves. Whatever our response, it is ours, and we can own it without allowing it to swallow us or define us. We have the freedom to fully experience a range of emotions, and to know at the same time that our emotions are not the limit of ourselves or of our world.

Grief is its own experience. Allowing ourselves the time and space to move through it is a commitment to ourselves and to honesty beyond what many of us have experienced before. The feelings move to their own rhythm and on their own time, and it can be very difficult to imagine that we are not "doing it wrong" when we are surprised by a wave of emotion at an inconvenient moment. As with so much of what we experience in recovery, there is no one way, and certainly no right way, to go through it. We take comfort in the knowledge that all things must pass, that our feelings will certainly change, and that others around us who have also grieved deeply find a way to survive their emotions, and to thrive once more. We find in recovery that even the worst things we experience can be transformed into a lesson we learn, and then a tool we can use to help others.

When we seek conscious contact with a power greater than ourselves, we find ways to be of service. Inside or outside NA, being of service helps us find value in our lives when we can't see our value for ourselves. Giving generously of ourselves, especially when we are in pain, is a path through some of our sorrow and confusion.

We often hear members share that "every day I am in recovery is a bonus," that "I have been given a reprieve." We have a deadly disease and are lucky to be alive—and even luckier to be glad we are alive. Many of us experienced in addiction a kind of living death, in which each day was a burden to be survived somehow. Many of us have suicide attempts behind us; whether or not we actively tried to take our own lives, we certainly held them cheap.

It can surprise us, then, how shocked we are when we receive bad news from a doctor. Our perfectly human reaction can seem to us like we are ungrateful or unrealistic. Again, giving ourselves permission to feel whatever we feel is as important as it is difficult. Only by admitting our feelings can we begin to deal with them, after all. Once we start talking about our feelings, their power over us is reduced. One member who had been through a series of medical crises said, "I don't know if I have a day or a decade left, but I would rather not spend it in fear." As we use the tools that are available to us, we find solace. The same tools that guide us to live lives we can be happy with can help us to walk the end of our journey with dignity and serenity.

Of course, not all of us know it's coming when our lives end, and some of us have many false alarms or close calls. Sometimes these brushes with death can be a wake-up call, allowing us to consider on a practical and spiritual level what it might mean to get our affairs in order.

In moments of great pain, a deep stillness comes over us; in those moments, we can see the depths of the darkness within us but also the enormity of the power to which we are connected. The terrible grief we feel can bring us a conscious contact that nothing else ever could. The impulse to withdraw, to pull away from noise and crowds and even from the people who support us the most, is often a form of self-protection: We can be so afraid of shaking loose the feelings again that we barely want to move. But letting the people we trust come and support us reminds us that we are not alone, even in our coldest moments. And allowing people to help us can be a form of service to them as well: When we let someone love us at a vulnerable time, they—and we—are rewarded. The caring and sharing we talk about is a two-way street, and those of us who are practiced at giving often have a hard time letting others love us back.

It is a loving act to let others love us. When we find ourselves in a position of need, it can be too easy for us to experience it as humiliating or burdensome. But we are given the opportunity to let those who love us express that in very concrete ways. The vulnerability we experience allows us a different experience of love. It is an act of generosity to let people be close to us, and we try to understand that they, too, are going through feelings about what's happening. Our training in letting go of self-obsession helps us now: As we help our loved ones through their fear and sadness, we may find the words we need to hear to get through our own grief and pain.

Certainly, as we recognize that we are loved and cared for, we realize that our lives really are different from what they had been: We matter in the world; we have made a contribution to the people around us and to people we can't see. The love we've shared, the families we've been part of, the meetings we've started and served and shared in—all of these have been a form of amends, a way of making peace with ourselves and our world. We are grateful for what we have and what we have had, and we know better than most people that death is not the worst alternative. We have seen others suffer worse fates, and perhaps we have ourselves. For some of us, in the surrender that comes after very bad news, we find that we are finally able to let go and be present in the moment. Letting go of the fear, the anger, and, gradually, the things that bind us into our lives, we are set free.

Courage

The serenity to accept the things we cannot change often comes after having had the courage to change the things we could. It takes courage and humility to open new doors and to close old ones. For many of us, courage was not something we came into the rooms with, but we find it here. We might still be afraid, but that no longer stops us from showing up and meeting challenges head-on. When we walk through our fear, our fear turns into faith.

Ultimately, this chapter is all about courage: the courage to accept the things we cannot change and to change the things we can, to look at ourselves as we are and accept ourselves anyway, to talk about things that make us uncomfortable, and to take on some of the issues that challenge us most deeply.

Working a program in relation to the physical part of our recovery does not necessarily mean working a physical program, though for some of us it does. We don't all take on exercise or proper eating or conscious physical healing as part of our daily program, though some of us make this a central part of our recovery. The principles are what we share, even when our practices are very different. We all find that it is necessary, sooner or later, to face the truth about our bodies, whatever that might be; to address the harm that's been done; to treat what we can, and surrender the rest; and to be honest. What we gain is acceptance of our physical reality, the ability to live as fully as we are able, and the willingness to do so—on life's terms.

5

Relationships

Recovery doesn't happen in a vacuum. We need one another, and we need to be involved with the world around us in order to recover. Living clean is all about relationships—with ourselves, with our loved ones, with our fellow members, with society, and ultimately with our Higher Power. The people in our lives are the means by which we experience grace. We see the miracle of change in others, and they reflect our own changes back to us. They are windows through which we see the world, and vehicles by which we achieve spiritual progress.

The truth is that most of us have not been very good at relationships. Some would say that an inability to form or maintain long-term relationships is one of the symptoms of addiction. The Basic Text tells us that the disease makes us "devious, frightened loners," that we develop strange habits and lose our social graces. When we came into recovery, we didn't always recognize what was wrong with the ways we related to people. Our experiences as using addicts shaped our habits and our expectations.

We have not been easy people. We do harm when we are using, and the people who are closest to us get the worst of it. We can be stubborn and suspicious, angry and afraid, sarcastic, willful, and set in our ways. We have been through hell, and we have put others through hell, too. We've experienced loss and failure and often violence. Even if we come in with families or careers intact, we need to change how we deal with them. Gaining these skills in recovery can be a long and sometimes painful process. When we look back on our active addiction and see the harm we caused, the relationships we destroyed, and the opportunities for intimacy we threw away, we may be overwhelmed by the wreckage. But we can also find some gratitude for the fact that we are clean now and we are changing. Our history with relationships can lead us to think that there is no hope for us in this area, but our experience with the Second Step proves to us that we can be restored to sanity. We need help that our loved ones cannot give us. The therapeutic value of one addict helping another really is without parallel. Caring and sharing the NA way is the ultimate weapon against our alienating, isolating, destructive disease.

Serious work is required. The issues we need to deal with emerge in the course of our interactions with others in and out of NA. As we go about our lives, just being who we are, we begin to heal. While we are healing, we experience difficulties and conflicts. When we no longer have the drugs to blame, we begin to understand the part we play in our own struggles. When we see ourselves creating wreckage while clean, we have a harder time making peace with ourselves. Some of us struggle to believe that lasting change is possible. Members who care about us will help us to see the ways we are still creating our own problems, but it's our responsibility to do something about it.

We learn to share, and share intimately. For many of us, sponsorship is our first honest, functional relationship—at the very least, the first in a long time. Sponsorship can serve as a model on which we begin to build other relationships that are healthy, loving, and productive. Many of our longtime members recall that they were "impossible" newcomers—questioning, doubting, arguing, and admitting their reservations. We made mistakes in public and dealt with the consequences. We built our foundation not by pretending, but by going through the struggle honestly and courageously, and accepting help along the way. Recovery is not always a tidy process; we are building intimate relationships with other people and with a power greater than ourselves, and neither of these comes naturally to all of us.

We don't all come into NA alone: Many of us come into recovery with partners, children, parents, and others we are close to. But many of these relationships have been damaged by our disease. As we recognize that we can't fix it all at once, it can be tempting to just walk away. But relationships are not like drugs, even though we may have used them for the same purposes; we can't simply abstain. The real work of living clean happens when we are in the world, relating with others. Our only choice is to learn as we go. We learn to deal with our family, our workplace, and our community at the same time that we are learning to find our place in the rooms. Each relationship we have affects every other. Each one teaches us things that help in the rest of our relationships.

We don't get long-term recovery without having relationships, both in and out of the rooms. It's the meat and potatoes of life—and the dessert! Relationships affect everything we do and everything we are. The ways we respond to our experiences shape who we become. When we are willing to stay in recovery, to allow ourselves to grow and change, we experience a full range of emotions. That we get clean at all is a miracle. But it doesn't stop there: We grow to be steady, reliable, loving people who can be a force for change in the lives of other addicts and beyond.

Relationships are central to everything we do. There is no step or tradition that is not somehow about relationships, and all of our literature talks about relationships in some way or another. There is no other area in our recovery that causes us more pain or more joy; it's where we see our growth and our recovery most clearly.

Fellowship

When NA began, the simple idea that addicts could recover in society, rather than having to be removed from it for long periods of time, was radical. For many of us today, what is revolutionary about our recovery is the love and intimacy we experience with other members. We come together in fellowship. As we stay together, we find in one another a deep affection and trust that can override the hurts and squabbles we have along the way. The ties that bind us together are also the roots that nourish our growth.

When our first surrender happens in the arms of NA, there is a connection that is made between the suffering addict and the fellowship. We know from the beginning that NA is our lifeline. When something else brings us ashore, we may not know that as clearly. It can be frustrating when we need to teach someone that NA is not an extended aftercare program or a treatment feeder. People get clean here, and we stay clean here.

Part of what makes unity so vital to our recovery is that it can be easy to forget how similar we are. Even after we have been here for a while, we can see our differences as separating us, rather than bringing us the freedom we need to grow into ourselves. It's one thing to reach out to a newcomer we hardly know, but when we have known each other for years and still don't care much for each other, it may take a little more effort to reach across the divide. We can see that a personality that doesn't appeal to us may still be able to carry the message to someone we couldn't reach ourselves. Having concern for each other in spite of our personal feelings can bring us surprising rewards. When we find ourselves caring about someone we don't like or don't know, we can feel our shared humanity, and we recognize a new level of spirituality in ourselves.

We call Narcotics Anonymous a fellowship for a reason: We are a community of equals. We are brought together by necessity, but when we keep coming back we find a common bond. We have a choice not only about whether or not we are members, but also about what our membership means to us, and how we experience or demonstrate it. As our connection with others develops, we move from being abjectly alone to being deeply connected. Some say that "NA" for them stands for "never alone, never again." Connection changes us, and the fact that we are all bound by a deadly disease means that the stakes are higher. The gratitude we feel at seeing a fellow member stay clean is not abstract. We may be grateful to have had a person as our friend for many years—but the fact that we have lost so many along the way means that we are grateful in another sense. Our friendship is also a celebration of our survival. Connected by our common disease and our primary purpose, we share a common bond unlike any other.

From the moment we come to the door of an NA meeting, our experience is about relationships. The welcome we receive as a newcomer has a way of staying with us. Many of us share about being treated like a human being for the first time in years when we came to a meeting: "That first meeting was the first time in a long time that someone treated me like a person, and not like a problem or a project." The fact that people greeted us, sat with us, even hugged us without wanting anything in return, seemed more surprising than the message we heard in words. "That wordless language of recognition, belief, and faith which we call empathy" is exactly what we need, and it happens in the exchange between virtual strangers in our meetings. This is nothing short of a miracle. Over time, we learn that we have a safety net we can trust, and we can rely on the people who care for us to carry us through.

Relationships are one area where we show our differences most sharply. Some of us stay pretty isolated, while others are surrounded by people; some of us develop large and vibrant social circles within the fellowship, while others of us have just a few friends we are comfortable with. Some of us find that in recovery we calm down in all kinds of ways, while others are still partying 'til dawn—but doing it clean. Some of us stop dating when we get clean, and others go a little wild. There is probably no area of recovery where we offer more advice, or take less of it. But the things we all have in common across the fellowship have little to do with any rules or advice; they have to do with the nature of our disease, and the tools we use to address it. What we share is the disease of addiction and the principles of recovery that can guide us in all our affairs.

There are some things that apply to all of us. We have a disease, and the core of that disease is self-obsession. The most important tool we use in fighting our disease is empathy: the sense that others understand us in a deep way, and the concern we feel for others that allows us to get out of ourselves and connect to something greater. Empathy means we get each other; we see the hidden darkness and love and hurt, and we understand. That is different from brutal honesty: taking the truth about someone and using it as a weapon to hurt them. Empathy is not emotional violence. We might hand one another the truth on a plate—unavoidable, obvious, terrifying, and maybe also kind of funny—but we don't use the truth as a means to gain power or humiliate. We show one another through our insight and example that we have a better self, and that we can rise to it.

The things we complain about most in the fellowship are often the challenges from which we learn the most. As much as we would like to imagine that we would learn to practice spiritual principles by reading about them, we learn what they mean and how to apply them by bumping up against each other, sometimes roughly. Sometimes simply not escalating a conflict can be a success. It may not be within our power to make peace, but we can certainly keep a situation from impacting the newcomer or the atmosphere of recovery we all treasure. Many times we have seen members who actively dislike each other set aside their differences to help a newcomer, or at the bedside of a sick friend, or at a moment of distress. The life-and-death struggles we experience and bear witness to put everything else into perspective. The conflicts, the drama, and the breakups in the rooms help to wear away our rough edges. We learn to deal with each other in spite of our feelings and our history.

The intensity of fellowship is what brings us from our condition as isolated, alienated, and frightened addicts to loving, caring, and sharing members of NA. When we are in the middle of the worst kind of conflict, we may struggle to remember that we are still welcome in meetings, that we still have people whom we trust and who care for us, and that we are still very much in the middle of the fellowship and of our own recovery process. We learn that when we have a genuine need or concern, almost any member will reach out to help, even if there has been some unpleasant history between us. We start to believe that we are safe. Over time, as we care for people and see that they really do support us, we start to feel a little safer. We can be a little more willing to take a risk, let go of what's not working, and try something different. Each time we make ourselves vulnerable and find someone there for us, we come to a new level of safety and trust.

We often tell newcomers we will love them until they learn to love themselves. What we are doing is loving one another back to life. That's true no matter how we express that love. Some of us are warm and affectionate, some of us are gruff and removed, but what we do in the rooms when a meeting is happening is the same. We are turning our attention outside ourselves and making a new kind of connection. The Basic Text tells us that love is "the flow of life energy from one person to another." This is essential to what we do. We connect with others, and through them, to a power greater than ourselves. Opening up to the world around us is a spiritual awakening.

One of our earliest connections in recovery is usually with a home group (whether we call it that or not)—a meeting we connect with and attend regularly. We look at members of the group who share a bond with one another, and we want what they have. We get to know others who are new and struggling, and we care about whether they make it back the next week. We start to hope for other members, and we find hope for ourselves as well. We find ourselves genuinely excited to see people celebrate their cleantime. We are interested in others. Practicing selflessness gives us relief from self-obsession. Caring about others and realizing that people care about us is another awakening.

Our spiritual awakening shows in our actions. We join a group, find a sponsor, take on a service position. We make commitments to show up and take action on a regular basis. We learn new ways to show our gratitude at the same time that we learn to be accountable. When we make a commitment, we learn to accept responsibility, to stick and stay through the hard parts, to do the best we can, and to ask for help when we need it. We learn our limits through over commitment, try to figure out the responsible way to let go, and find out it's okay to make mistakes. We learn that adversity, even conflict, is not the end of the story. We may do service for ego to begin with, but we learn through difficulty to be selfless, and that's the goal. We become part of something greater than ourselves. For most of our lives we were in the business of tearing down. What a joy it is to be part of something that not only saves people's lives, but makes them worth living.

The desire to serve comes from this sense of care and concern—and it is important to note that service is not limited to what we do inside the service system, or even inside NA. In whatever form it takes, service is what we do to act on our concern for others. In meetings, that might mean setting up chairs or helping to clean up afterwards; it could mean taking time to talk with an addict who is struggling or in pain, giving someone a ride to a meeting, or making sure that others feel included. Reaching out is the way we break out of our self-obsession. Service opens us to transformation and to love. The more we practice selflessness, the easier it becomes, and the more rewarding we find it to be.

Friendship

We may choose the first people we get close to in recovery just because they are available, or they go to the same meetings we do. When we are in crisis, it doesn't matter if we trust someone or not; we reach out and are grateful that anyone is there to grab our hand and pull us back from the edge. We need to trust before we begin to discern who is trustworthy. Discernment comes from hard experience: trusting people we shouldn't, being hurt, and coming back anyway. As our respect for ourselves grows, we choose more carefully whom we confide in. We get to know each other better—but we also get a better idea of ourselves and what we want and deserve in our friendships. We begin to recognize the elements of a healthy relationship. A sense of safety can be the biggest difference in our relationships. We start to feel like we can trust people, and we become more trustworthy ourselves.

Our Third Tradition teaches that we are all accepted in NA. We are not going to be thrown out if we make a mistake. So we get to experience different types of relationships—and different kinds of conflicts—safe in the knowledge that we will still be welcome when it's over. One of the things we notice in recovery is that we have many different kinds of friendships. We get to experiment with that, too, and find the ways we are most comfortable connecting. Those also change over time. Relationships are fluid, and that is part of what makes them so challenging: They change all the time. A member we have sort of known for years will ask us to coffee and we become fast friends—or we notice that someone we once were close to has grown away from us and we no longer seem to have as much in common. Our expectations about what a friend should be (or what a partner, a sponsor, or a parent should be) can keep us from addressing the reality of our relationships.

We let go of the things that cut us off from other people and from ourselves. The steps and traditions help us learn how to practice principles, and to clear away the mess that makes it so hard to see what is real. "There were parts of me that were frozen because of my childhood damage," explained one member. "I made a decision that no one would hurt me again and I would rely only on myself. It created a very lonely world: There wasn't room for anyone else, not even my Higher Power. It took some serious stepwork to recognize how my early relationships set the patterns for later ones."

The core of our disease is self-obsession. It needs to be dealt with from the very beginning of our recovery and for the rest of our lives. We begin to learn this the first time we walk into a meeting and feel we are in the right place: The identification we feel, the sense that other people know what we have suffered, breaks the grip of that self-obsession and frees us from ourselves.

Escaping the trap of self-centeredness opens us to others, and we are startled by their gifts and their uniqueness. We are each stronger in some ways and weaker in others. We find that we are able to help and be helped by the same person. They need what we have, and we need them as well. We awaken to a world where no one is simply what we think they are. Everyone has stories and struggles, assets and shortcomings. We can learn from anyone and everyone. Escaping from cycles of victimization, blame, and shame allows us to see how many other ways we are connected to the people around us—even those we don't yet know.

The gifts of recovery are available to us all, and they come through us all. We feel one another's joy and sorrow, we see one another's growth, and we genuinely want to help one another, even if there is nothing in it for us. Empathy is the ability to connect with others at the level of the heart and the spirit. Learning to develop empathy requires that we develop a conscience and a consciousness outside of ourselves. We develop care and concern, and in some cases even love for people without wanting anything in return. Empathy helps us to meet each other where we are.

There is a paradox here: We need to develop empathy and concern for others, and to let go of self-obsession without losing sight of ourselves. We can swing from one extreme to the other, from self-obsession to self-neglect and then back again. When we find ourselves caught in this pattern, we may be full of resentment and frustration. When we step back and do some inventory, we can see that our willingness to disappear into someone else's needs was not selflessness at all, but rather a reach for control—being indispensable makes some of us feel important, just as being taken care of does for others. When we let go of selfishness and self-centeredness, we don't lose who we are; we enhance it. There is always more room for empathy and greater capacity for love. We come to understand that just being ourselves really is enough to be loved and cared for by others and by a power greater than ourselves. We all have the opportunity to experience this freedom, but it takes some of us longer than others. We move in and out of self-centeredness as we learn to distinguish among our needs, desires, and fears.

We find our kindred spirits in the rooms—people who just plain understand us. We laugh at each other's jokes and at our experiences. Once we get comfortable with the changes in our lives, we can see the humor in many of the big issues we face in early recovery. But when we are still in the process, it is not funny at all. Our friends in recovery help us to laugh at ourselves. They may build us up and tear us down, but ultimately they accept us as we are. The friendships we share in recovery are among the strongest we ever experience.

Some of us use the word "family" to describe this closeness, and sometimes it really can feel that way—when we have holidays together, share celebrations and mourning, watch the big game together, and so on. One member suggested that a home group was like a family not only in its closeness, but also because we don't get to preselect its members: "Some of them are really difficult," she said, "but they're ours, and we love them." Some of us do have relatives who are in the rooms or are involved in our recovery, and our fellow NA members may be part of the lives of our children, our parents, our spouses. A member whose mother was elderly and alone brought Mom to all the local NA events, and she quickly became "Mom" to a whole group of people in recovery who were longing for family connections.

Some people regard the whole fellowship as a family, and there are usually one or two in an area who will say, "Hi family," when they begin to share. But some of us are uncomfortable with this. Especially if our own families were violent or unsafe, or if we have experience in other kinds of groups that made demands of loyalty from their members, the talk of "family" makes NA seem dangerous in those ways: that demands will be made of us, that we will be asked to compromise ourselves or put ourselves in harm's way for "the family." To some of us, it's not threatening at all—it just sounds a little cheesy. We may not even have language to describe the kinds of connections we have in NA, especially after we have been around for a while.

We walk with each other through the day-to-day struggles of our lives: romance and heartbreaks, births and deaths. Our sense of connection deepens into kinship. We may not always have the kind of intensity in our relationships that we do in our first few years, but the depth that grows in its place is also beautiful. When those people who are part of our early recovery continue to be part of our lives, time adds something to those relationships that nothing else can. We have long friendships that have weathered terrible storms, people we see twice a year but who pick up where we left off as if no time has passed, people who save our lives and we don't see them again for a year or a decade, people who are woven completely into our daily lives. These are deep emotional connections that exceed what we think of as friendship but don't quite match what we mean by family, either.

As we stay clean and build longstanding relationships, we experience a kind of safety we could not have imagined before. We know one another as well as anyone knows us. We have watched each other grow up and grow old, and in the lines on one another's faces we see the laughs and struggles we have shared over all that time. We may be incredibly close at some times and further apart at others, but there is something about just knowing we have each other that makes us feel a little less alone in the world. That love and connection feels as deep as any we have experienced.

The ways that we love in recovery can be intense and beautiful. We learn to love others—not just our fellow addicts, but our families and those around us—with a power we might never have imagined. Many of us turned away from love in our addiction. Those who loved us just made us feel ashamed. In our self-obsession, there was no such thing as enough, and the ways we were loved never seemed adequate to our ever-growing needs and demands. When there was sufficient care, concern, and support, we exploited it. Some of us were raised in addicted households, or in other circumstances where we never really felt love at all—or where it would come and go so randomly that we learned not to trust it.

Relationships are always evolving, and we are continually in new territory as our relationships grow and deepen. There will always be mistakes. Being able to recognize errors, clean them up, and move on is a gift of the Tenth Step, and it's not just that we are able to keep small problems from getting bigger. We struggle with the belief that we're not good enough. Minor problems in a relationship can magnify our sense that we are inadequate, unlovable, or unworthy. Even with many years clean, we alternate between avoiding responsibility for a problem and believing that it's all our fault. Surrender frees us from the feeling that we must constantly make up for being so awful. We can deal with our part, surrender, and let go of the rest. Accepting that we make mistakes and that they are not the end of the world or the end of a relationship is part of coming to terms with our own humanity.

We can share honestly who we are. Beyond our addiction, we are human beings: members of society who have gifts and flaws like everyone else. We are capable of loving and being loved, of caring for others and contributing to their well-being. In the process we build relationships with ourselves, our fellow members, and our Higher Power. "In the end, what is happening is that I feel loved and supported while learning to have honest relationships, without secrets or manipulation. Secure in the love of the fellowship, my heart is unfreezing."

Bridging Two Worlds: Relationships Outside NA

Our NA relationships might not be like any other relationships we have, but that doesn't mean they are the only relationships in our lives, or even the only important ones. We have family and friends outside the fellowship. Our jobs generally bring us into contact with others; many of us go back to school, or find other ways to pursue our goals personally and professionally. We develop interests and skills that have nothing to do with recovery, except that without recovery it's likely we wouldn't pursue those interests. In pursuing our passions, our careers, or our hobbies we make connections with the world beyond our doors in all kinds of surprising ways. Some of us are part of faith communities or other organizations that have their own ties that bind. In all of these relationships we learn and grow, practice principles, and try new ways to deal with old feelings. Our anonymity may be something we must guard carefully in order to maintain our place in those worlds.

Earthlings, normies, civilians—we use these terms to separate ourselves from people outside the rooms and mistakenly reinforce our own alienation. We struggle with the fear that if we get too integrated into the outside world, we will slip away from NA. Each of us seeks our own balance that allows us to participate in the world without sacrificing our recovery or putting ourselves at risk.

With a base of intimacy and safety in the fellowship, it can be easier to venture out into the world. Learning to live and serve by the traditions gives us particular skills that are very welcome outside the rooms. Willingness, honesty, belief in unity, and faith in the process make us valuable wherever we choose to serve. We know how to make ourselves useful, how to be teachable, and how to show respect and allow others to speak. Being able to focus on a primary purpose and work creatively toward it is so much a part of our way of life that we may not realize how highly valued that is in the world at large. Learning to serve gives us skills to lead. But it's in our relationships inside NA that a particular kind of work happens, and that's one of the reasons that it is so important for us to "plug in" to the fellowship.

With all of our talk about NA as "the last house on the block," or the place we need to be, or the place where we are always welcome no matter what, we sometimes lose track of what a beautiful thing we have. When we allow others to see our recovery and what it means to have a fellowship in our lives, we are sometimes surprised at how attractive it is. It's not unusual for us to hear a nonaddict sigh, "I wish I had what you all have." They can see the beauty of the gift, but they may not understand the stakes in our membership, or what we had to go through to "earn our seat." If they are fortunate, they will never understand that. We can be glad for their good fortune even as we are grateful that we have what we do.

We learn to care and share with others. Even though the boundaries can be very different with people outside, the principles we learn in our recovery can be practiced in all our affairs. Honesty and sincerity are almost always appreciated. We sometimes think that we have the market cornered on pain, but other people have their stories too.

When we share with them we discover that we have much to learn from one another.

Family

Our relationships with our families can present some of our biggest challenges. There is never only one set of feelings about our family members. There are times when we see our childhood only through rose-colored glasses, and other times when we forget that there was any joy or value there at all. The list of real and imagined hurts on both sides can be hard to get past. Whether or not they are still in our lives, our relationship to our family is a critical matter for most of us.

If we have an ongoing relationship with our families, we may not be able to wait until we get to the Ninth Step to handle all of the difficulties in those relationships. Whether or not we ever make formal amends to our families, we deal with the consequences of our actions—and the consequences of our recovery—every time we see them.

Amends means change, and our relationships with our families do change in recovery. Some of us choose to put some new distance in there. One member recalled that he had to move away for a while: "They were nice people, but I had to find out who I was, and I couldn't do that inside my family." Another member found that amends meant not tolerating abuse anymore, and felt she finally had permission to step away from a destructive household.

On the other hand, as we recover, many of us desire much closer relationships with our families than we had before. We enjoy our family, and the ability to be present and participate as a healthy, responsible member of the family is its own reward. What we learn about membership in NA can apply to our families as well. When we show up with an open mind and a willingness to be of service, the rewards can be far greater than our efforts. Sometimes those are the direct rewards of finding loving and productive relationships with the people we care for. Even when the rewards are not so direct, we can see them over time: Amending our behavior is something we do not to get a response from others, but to change our own relationship to ourselves, our Higher Power, and the world around us. As we learn to show up without anger, resentment, or fear, we develop an emotional maturity that we might not have expected.

It is a challenge to let go of old ways of being with our families, especially when those ways operated to our advantage. Sometimes NA service gives us a window on our patterns at home. We may see ourselves playing the same roles as elsewhere in our lives: We are acting as the victim or rescuer, the mediator or instigator. Sometimes it's positive and sometimes it's not. But the ability to see these patterns in one area of our lives allows us to change our behavior in all of our affairs.

When people are used to rescuing us or taking responsibility for us, it can seem simplest just to let them continue. As we take our own inventory, we can see the price we pay for not taking responsibility for ourselves in our relationships, our careers, and, most of all, in our spirits. Slipping the knots on our dependency on others can be done without needless harshness. We are grateful for the people who try to help us, whether or not we accept their aid. We try to keep in mind the wisdom of the Seventh Tradition: "Everything has its price, regardless of intent." We do our best to accept help when we need it, and to pull our own weight when we can. There is great freedom in taking responsibility for ourselves. We are able to look ourselves in the eye, and to be clearer about our motives.

After many years of recovery, a member found herself in the position of caring for her parents, with whom she had had a hard time as she was growing up. "Recently it has become clear how human and fragile they are," she said. "My feelings get hurt when my dad doesn't know who I am anymore, but in the larger picture it doesn't matter, because I remember who he is." Some of our hardest moments contain the keys to healing deep and painful scars. So often in recovery, the rewards come when we are not looking for anything but the next right thing to do.

We may be surprised to learn how many different ways people work through these things. Even if we seek professional help to address our childhood and family relationships, our recovery in NA does not need to be placed on hold. On the contrary, the basics of our program support us as we struggle with powerful feelings and memories. As other members share their love and compassion, we learn once more that we are not as alone as we feel.

When we take an honest look at our lives, we can see good and bad even in the most complicated families. The process of recovery offers us the freedom to choose what we want to bring forward from our past, and what we want to leave behind. It's not always as easy to do as to say, but the ability to make the decision greatly increases the likelihood of being able to carry it out. Our oldtimers sometimes remind us, "If you don't know what you want, you're not likely to get it."

Many patterns for relationships that have stayed with us through our lives were established early. We weren't born with all this damage. But we live with the events of our past, and some of them are traumatic. Abuse takes many forms, and not all of our history is easy to name. No matter which side of the equation we were on, the memories haunt us. Our history leaves us with issues that come up again and again: shame, fear, a belief that we need to justify our existence, and a sense of alienation from ourselves, our bodies, and other people. In our relationships this shows up as a feeling of failure before we even begin. It seems impossible for us to have a healthy, loving relationship, so the first sign of friction or tension seems to prove our worst suspicions. We escalate or walk away before our fears have a chance to come true—or be disproven.

Coming to terms with our experience happens over time, in layers: There are issues we must address immediately if we are to face life clean, and issues that we must develop a foundation in recovery in order to be able to face. The baggage that has traveled with us the longest is the stuff most likely to bring feelings of hopelessness. There are times we may be very frustrated to find ourselves facing the same issues that we had dealt with years before, but we find increasing freedom as we continue to chip away at them. When we are in the grip of an old pattern, we must remember our bottom line: Don't use, no matter what! There can be a long time between the work we do on a particular issue and our awareness that change has taken place.

For those of us with longstanding patterns of painful relationships, it can be surprising to notice the number of long-term, loving relationships we have in the fellowship.

Love sneaks up on us. The very fact of that love, and its undeniable presence in our lives, does its own quiet work healing the wounds that nothing else seems to reach.

Being a Parent

Perhaps nothing changes our perspective on our childhood like having children of our own. We gain a different perspective on our parents' experience, and we see ourselves through the eyes of our children as well. We want so badly to get it right—but we don't quite know what that means. Being a good parent might mean different things to each of us, but whatever we imagine it to be, we want to do it right. We can get so caught up in our theories and expectations of what it means to be a parent that we forget it's a relationship. All the things we learn about relationships in recovery can help us as parents—we see all the issues we struggle with in our other relationships show up in some form or other in our relationships with our children.

We learn to listen carefully, and to communicate in a way that we can be heard. Just as we do in sponsorship, we learn to meet our kids where they are. Perhaps most importantly, we learn that when we can get our self-obsession out of the way, we can experience love, compassion, empathy, and intimacy. As we make peace with ourselves, we find peace with those around us, including our children. When we practice self-acceptance, we can accept our children as the human beings they are. Perhaps the best gift we can give our children is acceptance of themselves. And since we cannot give what we do not have, what we want for our children can motivate us in our own journey.

Having children is a lifetime commitment, whether we enter into it carefully and thoughtfully or entirely by surprise. One of the things that distinguishes parenting from other relationships in recovery is that it is constant: We never stop being parents, even if we are not around our kids all the time. Whether we are with our children constantly or never see them at all, the fact that we are parents exposes us to a power of love we may not have known before. We are more capable—and more vulnerable—than we had imagined. Having children opens us to a deeper connection than any other in our lives, but it is also a lifelong lesson in letting go.

Many of us assume that being a parent is something we are supposed to know how to do instinctively, and it can be hard to ask for help. The principle of open-mindedness helps us to remain teachable, and to look for teachers all around us. Some of us find the support we need by bringing our children to meetings, and raising them immersed in the fellowship; others of us have children who have no idea we are in recovery at all. Whatever choices we make about how our families and fellowship intersect, we know that the skills we learn in recovery make us better parents, partners, and children to our parents at any stage of our lives.

There is a wide range of experience with being a parent in recovery. Some of us have our children with us through our addiction and our recovery; some start new families after we get clean; some of us never have children of our own, but become an important part of a child's life anyway. It's hard to talk about the experience without getting distracted by our different theories or beliefs about parenting, or even our different styles of communication.

We all have opinions about what's right and wrong. Recovery in NA gives us the freedom to figure out what is right for us and the chance to live it to the best of our ability. Just as there is no model of the recovering addict, there is no model of the recovering parent.

When we have responsibility for our children it can be very confusing to distinguish what is and what is not within our control. Writing an inventory helps us sort out what we believe so we can better act on it. "I was freaked out when I knew we were going to have a baby. I didn't have a clue what to do. My sponsor asked me to write about a few simple questions that were very helpful to me: What is a child? What are the needs of a child? What are a child's responsibilities? What is a parent? What are a parent's responsibilities?" Parenthood is one area where our self-centeredness can do real harm. Working a program of recovery keeps us from getting drawn into our self-obsession, and helps us to see when we are re-creating old patterns that we don't want to carry on to the next generation. Simply living lives of honesty and integrity sets a pattern for change. Our example teaches our children more than our words ever can.

If we have been separated from our kids for a while, we may need to get to know each other again as we learn to deal with each other. There is often a struggle when we reunite with our children; they have their feelings about what has happened, and it can be painful to acknowledge them. Our relationships with our children can be poisoned not only by the damage we do in our addiction, but by the guilt and shame we feel for what happened. Self-loathing is just another form of self-obsession, and blinds us to the needs of the person in front of us. When we get out of the way, we find that we can be good parents at any stage of our children's lives: Even if they are already adults, we still have something to offer them. Our experience with selfless service in recovery teaches us that if we show up with willingness, the opportunities for us to help will naturally appear.

"I let my kids take the lead on love. They showed me warmth and nurturance I hadn't known before, and I learned to stop controlling and just enjoy," another parent in recovery said. "My partner's big, warm family taught my child how to love and hug and call back. I am learning from him to accept their affection for what it is, even when it feels uncomfortable to me." Part of the joy and the difficulty of parenting is that we are constantly experimenting. No two children are the same, and no two parents are, either. We learn to adapt our beliefs to reality, check our behavior, and use the tools we learn in NA to build a family we are glad to be part of.

But even the best parents may have times when they are not so sure they like their kids. We are human; we are not our child's Higher Power, and there are times when just not doing the next wrong thing is the best we can manage. "I used to run into the bathroom and close the door," said one woman. "I'd get on my knees and just pray until the desire to hit my child would pass." Another said, "I would go in my room and just pray for bedtime." Our frustration and our fear can lead us to respond in ways we think we have grown past. We aren't perfect, but we are getting better. We start by not doing harm, and find that we can do a lot of good, if we are willing to try.

Having children while in active addiction is always hard. Generally, not even the worst parents mean to bring harm to their children, but in our addiction we harm them by what we do and what we don't do. Some of us did our best out there, but still came up short: "I thought being a good parent was buying my son fast food and toys with the money I got from stealing," said a member. In many cases, it seemed simpler for all involved if we just weren't around. We left our children with their other parent, with our relatives, or in foster care while we pursued our addiction, and found when we got clean that our desire to be a good parent was not enough to make parents out of us. Some of us were physically present but emotionally absent or unpredictable. Some of us know that we have done more damage than we can repair: "I was a lousy parent," one member said. "There's no denying it, and no way I can undo the harm. I will spend a lifetime making amends for it."

We know we harmed our own children, but we sometimes forget about the other children who were around us in our addiction: We babysat when we were using, or we ignored the neglect and abuse of children in the places where we used. If we cannot undo the harm, at least we can stop causing more of it. That in itself makes a world of difference. The program helps us stop doing damage, and then gives us opportunities to share our experience with others through meetings, sponsorship, and the power of example. We can break the cycles in our own families, and help others do better with their children as well.

On the other hand, some of us want to take responsibility for more than we could possibly control. We see our children struggling, and want to blame ourselves for their difficulties. We project the worst, based on our own experience. It's another kind of self-centeredness to see our child not as who he or she is, but as a reflection of ourselves, our parenting, or our decisions. "I thought my child was a little version of me," said one member. "I just figured we would like the same things and want the same things and think the same way. It took a terrible fight to learn that he's his own person, but I'm grateful. Now we are getting to know each other. He's not me, but he's someone I really like." Trusting that our children have their own path and their own relationship with a Higher Power can bring us to a new understanding of our own Third Step. When we get out of the way, our children come into focus as the unique human beings they are. Our recovery is a message to them and to us that there are such things as second chances.

Often we see signs of our own disease manifesting in our children, and it's not always clear whether they are just going through a phase or they are addicts like we are. We teeter between denial of what is happening and labeling any troublesome behavior as a symptom of addiction. Our desire to spare our children our experience can sometimes cause us to assume too quickly that we know what is best. Ensuring that our children have access to recovery might mean not pushing it on them too hard. Even for the people we love the most, this is still a program of attraction.

Many of us have lost our children in one way or another: They were taken from us, or we gave them up to ensure their safety, or something happened to them. For some of us, this is the deepest wound of our addiction, the loss we feel most acutely. With time and the tools of the program, we begin to heal, whether or not our relationship with them is restored.

If we are fortunate to have our children with us in recovery, we may find that our process and theirs really aren't that different: "We grew up alongside one another," said one addict. "I was as much a child as they were, and I had to be parent to us all. It's pretty embarrassing when your children mature faster than you do." We need help, we need advice, and we need the power of example. Turning to our friends in NA, the people in our communities, and the other adults in our children's lives, we find the tools and information we need. "I was a single parent, but I didn't do it alone," a member explained. When we are free to ask for help, we are able to acquire the tools we need to raise our children the way we believe is right.

Whether or not we come into recovery with families, we have a tendency to build them once we get here. Some of them look like the families we are used to—we find a partner and have children, or find a partner and share the children we already have. But we also put together families in other ways: We take in the children of family or friends who are not able to raise their own; we adopt or foster. We blend families in surprising patterns. "I was heartbroken when I learned that one of the consequences of my addiction was being unable to have children. A sponsee was sharing her stepwork with me, and she wondered aloud if the childless mother was here to mother the motherless child. It was as if a light went on—I looked around the rooms and there were these kids fresh off the streets who had no one, and it seemed like God's will for me was clear." Some of us end up taking care of elderly or sick friends who have no families of their own. However it happens, many of us find our homes full of love and full of people we love, whether or not we are related. The ties that bind us are not limited to those we first recognize when we come together in unity. Family can be a pretty hard concept for some of us.

We make peace with it one way or another, sometimes by reinventing it altogether.

Amends and Reconciliation

As our behavior changes, we no longer leave a path of chaos and damage in our wake. But we recognize there is no way to "unring" a bell; there are instances where the damage we caused may be difficult for others to forgive. Making amends is necessary to live free of the guilt, shame, and remorse that keep us trapped in self-destruction. But the process neither begins nor ends when we sit down with the person we have harmed to have that talk. With the help of our sponsor, we reconcile ourselves to the truth of what we did, and begin the process of making peace with the consequences of our actions. An honest relationship with ourselves and real, tangible change in our lives are necessary for amends to have much value. There is a reason we come to this work so late in the steps. The process is one of the most important we ever undertake, and we do not enter it lightly.

The direct amends we make in words are crucial to our recovery, but that's only part of the process. Living those amends means allowing the changes in our personalities and our behavior to become reliable and consistent in the lives of those we care about. We do this whether the people we care for are changing or not, whether they forgive us or not, whether our relationship becomes what we wish for or not. When we clean up our side of the street, we can feel easier in our hearts and spirits. But that by no means obligates anyone else to clean up their part, nor does it suggest that our families will magically transform into what we always wished they were. More likely, we learn to make peace with the families we have, and to accept the reality of who they are. We learn to meet them where they are without conditions or expectation.

There are some people who never forgive us. Often those people are members of our family. As dearly as we may want their forgiveness, the simple truth is, it's not going to come until they are ready. Living with that can be enormously difficult. The desire to fix it can be so powerful that we make things worse by not letting go and letting them heal in their own time. One member shared that twelve years after her initial amends, her daughter finally declared that she was forgiven. "It was grace that all those years I didn't know that she was still struggling with this," she said, "because if I had known I wouldn't have let go, and I don't know if we could ever have gotten there." Whatever we need to say to the people we have harmed, we know that the deepest amends we make is that we change. And while we can feel the depth of the change in our lives, people who struggled with us for years of our addiction may take a long time to trust or believe it. We may have trouble trusting it ourselves. We harbor that same doubt that the changes we are making will stick, and when others don't believe we have changed, we can fall into that trap with them. Having people who believe in us and in our recovery can be essential to walking through this process, especially when it's long. The reward can be a deep self-acceptance: We forgive ourselves, we forgive others, and we find peace—regardless of what others may think or feel or tell us. A member shared, "I am not who I was, no matter who is not convinced. That lie is dead."

Reconciliation is an important spiritual principle for us to consider: We come to terms with the reality of our actions, and we also reconcile with people we have had conflict with. Sometimes reconciliation means that we restore the relationship to its previous state, or to a new state based on current reality, and sometimes it means that we make peace with the fact that the connection with that person is lost. Reconciliation can also mean restoring balance—like when one "reconciles accounts." When we take on what is not ours, as when we take responsibility for someone else's feelings or actions, we are out of balance, and the result is often destructive. We do what we can to amend the harm we have done and to restore balance in our relationships, and we let go of the results. Facing the responses of some people from our past may give us a much sharper vision of who we had been, and it can take some work to make peace with that. We want to be very aware of who we are becoming, and use this new information about our past to help move us forward.

If making amends is about change, one change we can make is not to subject ourselves to abuse anymore. Finding the balance between hearing someone out and putting ourselves in danger is difficult. We are the only ones who can say where that line is, and we may not find it in the moment. Like so many things we work through and walk through in recovery, it comes in layers. It can be useful to know that addressing something once does not necessarily mean we are "done" with an issue, a memory, or an amends. More is continually revealed to us, and sometimes in the course of dealing with what we know we learn more than we had expected.

Walking with the knowledge that someone has not forgiven us is hard, but through it we find levels of forgiveness and acceptance that we may not have known were possible. It brings us to a clearer understanding of what the Ninth Step is for, and we learn to recognize the difference between hope and expectation. As much as we might want someone to forgive us or to own their part of a situation in which harm was mutual, we have no right and no reason to expect that. Sometimes the path to forgiving ourselves begins with forgiving another for their lack of forgiveness. As we forgive them, we may find compassion for the pain they experience at carrying that resentment—and for the pain we caused them in the first place. We understand that everyone's sense of harm is different. Something that we might find easy to let go of, someone else may find unforgivable: That is not our business to decide or to change. When we understand the gravity of the damage we did, we can see that accepting their lack of forgiveness may, in fact, be part of our amends. We realize, too, that forgiving us may have other consequences for the person to whom we are making amends. It may threaten their other relationships, or their sense of themselves. We are the only ones whose recovery we have any control over. We can only amend what is ours. The rest is out of our hands, and we practice letting go.

Miracles do happen, and we are not the only ones who experience healing. Sometimes reconciliation is possible, but not necessarily on our schedule or our terms. We practice forgiveness, patience, and acceptance. We must give time, time—even if it's a lifetime. In the meantime, we are surrounded by people who believe in us and care for us—and if we pay attention, there is always someone who needs our help. We can turn the love we feel toward those who welcome it, building and cherishing the relationships that are present in our lives today.

Romantic Relationships

The Basic Text offers a suggestion about romantic relationships: that we begin by writing about what we want, what we are asking for, and what we are getting. When we explore these simple questions, we begin to see how we can use the tools of recovery to change our behavior and our experience of intimacy. We learn to check our motives and to be honest about what we want; we begin to get free of our old baggage and experience relationships in the present tense. Practicing principles like honesty, courage, and faith opens us to the possibility of love, acceptance, and trust in our lives.

what we want

We often hear that if we made a list for ourselves in early recovery of what we wanted, we would be selling ourselves short. It's not just in the beginning that this is true—over and over, our dreams for ourselves are glimpses of God's will, not a road map. Many of us have found this in our romances, as well. We take on the project of finding a partner in much the same way we might shop for a new car: We make a list of the features we want or don't want, and begin evaluating available models based on our list. We may be surprised, on finding the one who seems to meet our criteria, when things still don't work out as we had planned.

Our sponsor might suggest turning that list back on ourselves, asking what it would take for us to become the person we imagine as a partner. Others might suggest stepping away from such a list altogether, thinking instead about what would constitute a relationship we would like to be in. Some of us are masters of projection: By the time we go on a first date with someone, we have already imagined the whole relationship, from steamy beginning to bitter divorce. Allowing ourselves to be present means that we can have a relationship with a person, rather than a fantasy. Learning to live in the moment frees us to enjoy ourselves. Applying skills like communication and active listening, practicing principles like unity, compassion, and sharing, we can learn to use the tools we need to be in a solid relationship long before we are actually there. These behaviors don't just make us more likely to get what we want; they also make us happier and more fulfilled where we are.

There is so much in the way of our ability to have the kind of relationships we want: fear, selfishness, reservations, the belief that it will just end badly. The more we take inventory, the more clearly we see the obstacles inside ourselves that stand between us and what we want. We may mistake our impulsiveness for intuition, and imagine that we have fallen in love as soon as we get excited. Or we might resist feeling at all. Not wanting to risk our hearts means that they never really get full. As we learn to open up, we also learn to survive being hurt. Strangely, as it gets easier to withstand that kind of hurt, it seems to happen less often. We choose better, come into relationships a little more cautiously, and learn to recognize and address signs of difficulty much sooner. Healthy relationships begin to replace the chaos that had consumed our lives. Sometimes we miss the chaos. Living without the drama and clutter of active addiction is strange. We may be compelled to create drama in recovery just so it feels familiar.

"Don't get into romantic relationships in your first year" might be the most repeated, least listened-to piece of advice in the fellowship. We need time to get our feet on the ground, to build support, to work some steps and figure out who we are, but many of us don't take that time in the beginning. This is like building a house without laying a foundation: Sooner or later that work needs to get done, and it's a lot easier to do it in the beginning than to try to build a foundation under a standing structure. Many of us who don't take that time in the beginning find that we need it later. If we survive that first breakup clean, we have a pretty good idea of what that time is for.

Not all of us take a full year, and some of us take much more time before we start dating. We may even find that we are happier and more serene when we are single, and choose to stay that way. Once we figure out that there is nothing to be afraid of and no one right answer, we can answer the big questions for ourselves and know we can always change our mind later, if we choose.

We want a magic formula that will make relationships okay: a year, three years, a Fifth Step, a round of steps. The truth is much simpler, but harder to define. Some of us are never "ready" and struggle all our lives. We know members who are scholars of our principles but have many failed marriages behind them; we also see newcomers stumble into a relationship and somehow make it work. When it works, we are happy to take the credit. When it doesn't work, we try to understand why. There are always lessons. Experience is what we get when we don't get what we want. But some lessons are so clear that we don't have to act out to learn them. With practice we develop personal responsibility, accountability, and discernment. Mostly we know when we are doing something wrong, taking advantage of someone who is vulnerable, being controlling, deceptive, or abusive—and we have a responsibility to ourselves as well as to the other person to stop it.

It can be hard to admit, but the times when we most desire to be in a relationship are often the moments when we are least equipped to handle one. So many of us struggle with the fear that we will never have a partner, and that not having a life partner means we will always be "alone." This kind of fear leads to panic—and to pain. When we are lonely, sad, or trying to distract ourselves, we may be willing to settle for things that are not actually what we want in the long term. When our priority is simply not being alone, we are likely to compromise our values or our priorities, to commit too quickly to a person we are just getting to know. There's an old saying, "Be careful what you pray for—you might get it."

We mistake intensity or sex for intimacy, and are likely to think something is serious when we've really just been seeking distraction and a fix. Or we settle for sex when what we really want is love. Afraid of being alone, we patch the emptiness we feel with a relationship. "He became my higher power and my drug of choice," said one member of the guy she dated when she was a newcomer. "I was calling all the time, when I was bored or lonely or happy, asking, 'What are you dooooing?' I was clean, with no tools and a new obsession. Nothing had changed." (That same member also reported that someone suggested to her, "If it's after ten at night and it sounds like a good idea—don't do it.") Sometimes it seems as if our latest drug of choice is another person. It can be surprising to discover that having a crush on someone turns so easily into self-obsession—but when we examine our thinking, we can see how concerned we are with whether we are being noticed and how we are being perceived.

Too often, we let our recovery take a backseat to a new relationship. We find ourselves missing meetings, calling other people less often, and not working as hard on ourselves. There is no reason to be surprised if the relationship suffers when we are not caring for ourselves, but it can feel like we are taking needed energy out of the relationship when we take the time and space we need to work our program. We do the work to become the kind of person who is ready for the relationship we want—but we have to keep doing the work to be that person inside the relationship, as well. "It's like pouring 'Miracle Grow' on your recovery," one member said. "If you want to get to know yourself, get into a relationship." "No," said another: "If you want to get to know your *sponsor*—get into a relationship!"

Some of us get clean and begin a pattern of apparently serious relationships that all end in calamity. The drama of falling in and out of love can be its own reward, and we seem to have the same relationship over and over with different people. The intensity of early love may be so compelling that we seek it again and again. Sometimes it's our behavior in the relationship that gets in the way, but we can also see trouble even before the relationships begin—we notice that we're choosing people who just aren't appropriate for us. We joke sometimes about having a "broken picker," but the reality can be pretty painful.

It's not surprising that some of us get strung out on sex. We want something to make us feel good, fast. Sometimes just the flirting is its own little high—we like playing the game. Making the connection is its own rush, even before anything "happens." That is not to say that it's a problem for all of us, or even for all of us whose relationship with sex is casual. Like so many things in recovery, it's not a problem until it's a problem for us. We may want to ask ourselves if sex is making our lives unmanageable, if it is contributing to our happiness or unhappiness, if obsession and compulsion are playing a part in our behavior, or if we're lying, keeping secrets, or sneaking around. We take an honest look at whether our behavior is hurting our loved ones—or if it would hurt them, if they knew about it.

We need to be honest about what we are doing. We may be looking for a meaningful relationship, or for a good time, or we may be looking for trouble. Understanding our motivation makes it a lot easier to understand our consequences. It's not that we always get what we ask for, but when we want one thing and ask for another, the consequences are usually disappointing. We can hardly hope to be honest and open with a partner if we are still practicing self-deception.

What matters is that we are comfortable with our behavior and our decisions. Other people have opinions, but we learn to identify what we want, what we believe, and how we choose to live. That can look very different from one member to another, or from one point in our lives to another. Behavior that was comfortable in early recovery may be unthinkable later on; or we may find after years clean that we feel a freedom to experiment that we never had in the beginning. It is entirely reasonable for our behavior to change as our needs, wants, and desires change; the issue is that we are clear about that with ourselves.

what we ask for

Over time, we find increased acceptance of ourselves and our circumstances. We learn to enjoy our own company, and to handle our own desires and responsibilities appropriately. It can be surprising when we notice that we no longer seem to "need" a partner as we once did. What is more surprising is how much easier it is to be comfortable with a partner once we know we want a relationship—but we don't need one. Having support in place means that we have some of the resources we need for a successful one-on-one relationship, but also that we have the help we need if things don't go as we had hoped.

Relationships are one area where practice alone doesn't make perfect. Some of the most important work we do to improve our relationships isn't done in those relationships at all, but with our sponsors and trusted friends. Even with many years clean, separating and reconciling what's in our heart and what's in our head doesn't come automatically. We need another set of eyes; we need a caring, attentive listener to help us sort things out. A good sponsor is a key to opening the possibility for change in the way we relate to others. That relationship can form the basis for all the rest of the relationships we have in recovery. Some of us are clean for a long time before we find a sponsor with whom we connect. We may find that listener in another trusted friend. Wherever we find the safety to begin, opening up about our experience is critical to change.

It is no secret that addicts have trouble accepting reality. This is no less true for us in our intimate relationships: We get tangled up in a fantasy of what our relationship is supposed to be, and lose track of what it actually is. When we love a fantasy, we get angry with reality. Anger with reality is the opposite of acceptance. We can get so involved with the fantasy of our partner that we are furious with them for not living up to that image. Sometimes the best we can do is to walk away, but often walking away is the easy way out. The journey is learning to accept the person we love in spite of all the ways they don't match our fantasy of who they should be or could be. It is possible that perfect unconditional love is something only a Higher Power is capable of, but as we get closer to achieving this ideal in our own lives, our spirits blossom. The more deeply we love, the more we are capable of loving. The more we open ourselves to grow through our relationships, the more intimacy we experience.

With many years clean, we may find that we appear mature, that in many ways our lives have begun to look the way we want them to—but we still struggle in our intimate relationships. Distinguishing mature from immature love can take as long as it takes to mature: It's a lifetime process. When we admit how much of the damage in our lives has revolved around sex and love, we can see how much can be gained by a restoration to sanity in this area. We work the steps to clear away the wreckage of our past; we use a sponsor to help us address the wreckage of our present; we use the traditions to learn new ways to get along with others. We are more generous and less selfish and fearful. We learn to have standards and limits, but also to be open: We can become so rigid in our demands that finding a partner becomes impossible. We let go of our expectations of others and we begin to ask a little bit more of ourselves.

Gradually we come to see where we need to change and where we need to stand firm in our beliefs, even if it means waiting. We start to see when our beliefs keep us safe, and when they drive us into the same patterns over and over. "I don't have a fear of abandonment," said one member. "I expect it." When we expect the worst, we usually get it. Learning from our experience is important, but being willing to believe we can move beyond it is also crucial. Giving ourselves and others permission to change also means surrendering to the possibility that we may find ourselves in strange territory: When we are not repeating the same relationship, we may feel like we don't know what to do at all. "It has taken many years," one member said, "but in my last Fourth Step it was suddenly clear that I didn't get involved with the same person over and over—I was the same person. It didn't matter who the other person was, I still reacted the same way." Doing something different is a risk—but making the same mistakes is a guarantee of failure. An oldtimer said it best: "We used to think we had trust issues, but now we know we have courage issues."

The more we experience freedom from active addiction, the more we can see how our addiction drives us into corners even when we are not using drugs. The ways in which we create damage in our lives or put ourselves in harm's way have a tendency to repeat. A little clarity may be all it takes to change an old and painful pattern. Sometimes we can see it all too clearly, and do it again anyway. We examine our motives and our willingness, we share about it, we fill notebooks with inventory—but there we still are, experiencing the same conflict in service that we did in our last job, or in the same relationship with a different partner.

It can be easy to judge one another when we see this kind of repetition, but the truth is, it's not over 'til it's over. Sometimes the pain just needs to be great enough; but sometimes, looking back, we can see that other kinds of healing had to happen before we were ready to deal with some of that deeply buried stuff. We may be disappointed to discover that our shortcomings are removed, but not in our order of preference. Each time we go through an emotional storm, we are given an opportunity to let go of more of the burden of the past and find more freedom on the other side. Our future is less and less determined by our history.

the courage to trust

There is no right way or wrong way to experience love. What matters is that we allow ourselves the privilege. We love whom we love. It doesn't always make sense or look good on paper. A happy couple put it like this: "The thing is, whether we love each other or can't stand each other on any given day, it's really fun. We can be playful, we can fight, we can come together and just enjoy each other's company. It might look a little fishy from the outside, but we're enjoying every minute of it." Perhaps we really have found our mate—or maybe there's a lesson it's time for us to learn. When we let go and allow others to be who they are, we are able to let go of our own insecurities a little more, and be honest about who we are. That's not a deadly serious proposition: We can be playful and silly, loving and tender, frightened or sad.

We can finally be free of that terrible sense we have that who we are isn't enough, or that if they really knew us, they'd leave.

Our relationship with ourselves determines the quality of our relationships with others. It seems so obvious, but in the moment it can slip away from us. When we're not feeling so good about ourselves, when we are hurting, when we feel lonely and insecure, of course we want someone else to tell us we're okay. But the better we know ourselves, the better we know our needs and what we have to give. "It helps if at least one person in the relationship knows at least one of the people in the relationship," a member explained, "but I've been a stranger to myself sometimes even when I wasn't new. Seeing into myself honestly and accurately is something that comes and goes. I find now I can name a lot of emotions, but that doesn't mean I know what I'm feeling at any given moment, especially when my feelings are strong. I still default to anger, depression, and resistance when what I'm really feeling is loneliness, desperation, or fear. It comes out sideways at the people nearest me. I comfort myself with the idea that I recognize it sooner than I used to—after a bad week, rather than a bad month or a breakup. But it still hasn't gone away." We can see the rewards of the Tenth Step when we start being able to recognize our emotions as we are having them. When we can identify our own responses we can choose to respond rather than react.

Practicing principles in our relationship doesn't mean being someone else, or being phony, but it can feel a little awkward at first. Our sponsor can be a great help to us as we begin to try new ways of responding or reacting. As we try to replace old, defective ways of thinking with new ideas and attitudes, issues arise that we may not have seen before. We are faced with choices and challenges we didn't see coming.

Being in a relationship is a different experience when we put unity first. When we set aside our own needs and consider the good of the partnership or the family as a whole, it does not mean that we tolerate our needs going unmet or unacknowledged. We start to recognize that each of us will get what we need if both of us come to the relationship with an attitude of willingness and a belief that when we allow our unity to be a priority we can turn the results over to a power greater than ourselves.

Self-support is a spiritual principle, and learning to support our own spirits is a critical part of our development. Of course, we don't just "go it alone." We have the group, we have our sponsor and trusted friends, and we have a Higher Power that helps us carry on. We share our triumphs and burdens with our partner, but learn not to make them responsible for our moods or the overall quality of our lives. When we can have a bad day without insisting our partner also be miserable, we know something is really changing. "The first time I came home angry, and my girlfriend started in, and I didn't say the next wrong thing, I knew a Higher Power was working in my life," said one member.

Learning the difference between having a partner and taking a hostage—or being taken hostage—is a big step for a lot of us. "Letting go of expectations" can be a nice name for letting go of control. Allowing our partners and ourselves to experience personal autonomy means we can grow and change at our own pace, and the relationship can benefit from what each of us brings to it. When we are willing to stand still and be present in a relationship even as it changes, or as we change, we come to understand commitment in a new way. Just as it's normal in recovery to sometimes think about using, sometimes in the closest relationships we may think about running. Standing still in spite of the impulse to run can be a great spiritual exercise. A sane solution is often possible if we are willing to wait for the answers we need. Open-mindedness is critical to getting through difficulties in our relationships.

Being with someone who is not in recovery presents particular challenges. One is that we may feel judged or excluded by our friends in the rooms. Too often we think of people coming in two types: *in* recovery and *needing* recovery. The very idea of a healthy relationship with someone who isn't "one of us" can seem unlikely. In fact, it's no more or less likely than being happy with someone who is in recovery. We may have to work a little harder to balance our priorities between our commitments to our partner and to our recovery. When we are out of balance, it can seem like we're leading a double life. We may find that the language we use to express ourselves or describe our feelings is not the same. Relationships require compromise and learning. In the rooms we find the tools we need to have the relationships we want in our lives. Outside the fellowship, we find ways to apply the principles without necessarily naming what we're doing. The flexibility that relationships require comes more easily to us when we are practicing principles in our lives. We learn to resolve challenges as they arise and to have the courage to say what we think and how we feel, even when it's uncomfortable. Willingness to change means that we can allow relationships to grow, cool off, or develop into something we hadn't imagined before.

When a relationship that's important to us isn't working, it can feel like nothing is working. Conflict with our loved ones can be traumatic, and a breakup with a lover or a friend can set off an overwhelming wave of emotions. Relationship troubles are hard for anyone, but for addicts they hold particular danger: The pain can be so great that using seems like an option again. If our friends in recovery seem to be taking sides, we can feel so alienated that going to meetings feels unsafe. That old triangle of fear, anger, and resentment can feel like an iron cage, and the antidote—connection to others—seems like the last thing we want. Taking care of ourselves in the simplest ways, like eating, sleeping, and going to work, can be very difficult when we are in pain. The newcomers around us can serve as powerful examples, reminding us to show up and reach out when we're hurting. Any member at any time is liable to save our lives.

We might find, after some consideration, that a relationship really does need to end. But we can do it in a way that we are comfortable with, instead of acting on impulse and leaving a painful mess to clean up later. Ending a relationship doesn't mean someone has to be wrong or bad; in fact, it can be the best thing for all involved. We can feel pressure to stay in a relationship—for social approval, the kids, complacency, or fear—even though we know it's time to go. It is an act of courage to do what we think is right without having to create damage to justify our actions. We no longer need to have an affair to end a marriage; we may have the clarity not to enter that marriage to begin with, or to exit with dignity and integrity. We let go of our schoolyard mentality and allow ourselves to be present with each other as adults, willing and ready to share the experience.

Sometimes as we are dealing with the loss of a relationship, we are surprised by the force of our feelings. Our reaction seems all out of proportion to the loss we are experiencing—and it may be. That's not a reason to judge ourselves or pretend it's not happening, though we may be tempted. There is no right or wrong about how we feel. Some of the feelings we didn't experience when we were using are still waiting for us when we get clean, and a loss in recovery can set off a cascade of feelings from all those earlier losses we hadn't grieved. Our sponsors can be a lifeline when we go through this kind of experience. If we are willing to hang on, trust, and do the work, we can find real healing in the steps. Relapse is a possibility, but so is making our lives unmanageable through gambling, shopping, sex, or eating—anything to push the feelings away. Some of us repeat this pattern for years in recovery before we are willing or able to push through the pain and take an honest look at what has been happening.

Our ideas about relationships are often based in anything but reality; we want to believe that relationships somehow happen on their own, that we can step into a relationship like it is a carnival ride and it will just take us. Just as we imagined the right combinations of drugs would make everything alright, we sometimes imagine that the right combination of attributes will make a soul mate. We place unrealistic expectations on ourselves and others. We fantasize and project about how things "should be." Partnership isn't found; it's built. We need to show up and participate in its construction. But once we start taking care of ourselves, all kinds of intimacy are available to us.

Conscious Contact

In NA it's not true that we can't love others until we love ourselves; in fact, that is exactly what we do. We experience empathy, and it grows into something greater. Gradually we build a relationship with ourselves as well, and we clean up the things that keep us in self-loathing and self-sabotage. We learn to love others, but our relationships with them are a struggle until we learn to have a relationship with ourselves and our Higher Power. In turn, our relationship with ourselves and our Higher Power is enriched and informed by our relationships with other people.

We learn to respect the spirit in one another. We all have our own ways of thinking and feeling. When we acknowledge that each of us is in the care of a loving Higher Power, we can accept one another where we are and see that each of us has our own path. If it is based in spiritual principles, it will serve as a good guide. Learning to step outside our own reactions and accept reality makes us more flexible and able to deal with the challenges that relationships present to us.

Because recovery is progressive, we continue to work steps and to reveal more about ourselves. We come to know our intentions. We get better at hearing our own voice, our own conscience, and listening to our instincts. Addicts who make it to recovery have pretty good instincts, but we've taught ourselves over time not to trust them. Learning the difference between the voice of our intuition and the voice of our disease is not something that can be explained; we figure it out in meditation, when we practice listening to ourselves and our Higher Power. We share our experience with our sponsor as it unfolds, and he or she points out to us when our instincts are serving us well. We become increasingly aware of our choices, our motives, and our behavior. We come to know what we were thinking when we made a decision, and we recognize the difference between thinking through to a decision and reacting or acting on impulse. Listening to our intuition means that we can be open to others without being naïve or foolhardy. We learn to trust our intuition and honor our feelings.

The conscious contact we speak of in the Eleventh Step is a relationship with our Higher Power. Intimacy is conscious contact with another human being. We connect. As we get close to others we see the divine in them, and we see it in ourselves as well. We pay attention to them, and to ourselves when we're with them. When we feel real joy at seeing a struggling member finally get that thirty-day keytag, when we find the words we didn't know we had in us, when we make a genuine connection with another human being and feel something shift inside of us—we feel love in action, flowing through us, changing us for the better.

Each of our relationships teaches us how to make our other relationships better, stronger, more meaningful—if we stop and listen for the lessons. And all of these relationships, in turn, bring us back to our relationship with ourselves. We cannot say that one is more important than another, any more than we could say one side of a pyramid is more important than the next. In fact, the pyramid that is in our symbol is made up of relationships: with self, society, service, and God. Rooted in a base of goodwill, these are the relationships that bring us to a point of freedom. Our capacity to love grows in proportion to the effort we make to show love, and our willingness to accept it. And with that capacity for love—something so many of us never even thought we wanted—we begin to feel that our lives have meaning and purpose. The harm we've done, the pain we've suffered, the loss we've experienced all deepen our compassion for others, and our understanding of their struggles. Our real value is in being ourselves, not in spite of what we have been through, but because of it.

A New Way of Life

Our literature tells us that we become "acceptable, responsible and productive members of ... society," but it also cautions, that "Social acceptability does not equal recovery." Both statements are true, but they are not mutually exclusive. We each measure being a productive member of society in our own way.

Our ideas of success are as individual as we are. We start at different places and our destinations are just as varied. We know how to do some things very well and others not at all. We may enter recovery with a career still in place, or it may be that getting a steady place to live is a big step. We have this in common: We want to be free. We want to feel accepted and respected without pretending to be anything other than who we are. No matter what our accomplishments, the principles by which we live will sustain or destroy us.

We progress in this journey by applying what we learn in recovery to the rest of our lives. Step Twelve calls this "practicing these principles in all our affairs." The freedom we are seeking is not some abstract thing. It's how we live. Our Basic Text goes on to tell us, "The steps do not end here. The steps are a new beginning!" NA offers us the principles that will transform us and the laboratory in which we practice applying these things before we take them into the world.

The work we do in the steps helps us to define our values and teaches us to work toward our goals. It doesn't matter how many times we have taken the steps; there is always something new in the work and in the reward when we do it to the best of our ability. But when we stop halfway through, we don't just miss half the gifts of recovery; we miss the point. Oddly, it's just when we come face-to-face with our most painful character defects that we stop surrendering. Our commitment to work the steps has consequences whether or not we follow through. When we stop in the middle, we leave ourselves with too much awareness and not enough hope. When we see the process through, we notice that *doing* the work takes much less energy than *avoiding* the work.

We surrender, accept ourselves in the moment, and graciously allow our lives to unfold. Finally, we can stop seeking the piece of the puzzle that will make it all okay. We practice living a principled life, and our journey into the world shapes itself from there. We let go of our fear of change and come to realize that we are all changing all the time. We can embrace that change and truly believe that we can stay clean no matter what. The process gets simpler; doing the right thing comes more naturally.

We try new things, exploring deeper layers inside and higher levels outside. As our values change, we change our lives. The process is like a spiral staircase. Again and again we come to the same view, only each time we are seeing it from a different perspective. Being open to one another's viewpoints helps us to clarify our own thinking. When we put love, effort, and commitment into action, our lives miraculously change.

Moving Beyond "Social Acceptability"

When we get here, we are told that "we are not interested in...who your connections were, what you have done in the past, how much or how little you have, but only in what you want to do about your problem and how we can help." Years down the line, this statement remains true. No matter where we are heading, we go about building our new lives in the same ways. With time we learn that how we get there matters more than the destination itself.

One of the benefits of our experience is that we know our participation in society is a choice. How we engage with the world around us is our decision. Whether or where we want to fit in is our decision, too. Integrating into the world in a way that is comfortable for us is part of our journey, not the destination. Finding our place in society isn't the goal; it's a means by which we achieve our goals. The idea of achieving social acceptability can distract us from the goal of awakening our spirits.

Many of us ask ourselves to what society we want to be acceptable. Some of us understand "society" to be NA itself. We find a way to make ourselves at home in NA, even if we have always been loners, skeptics, and outsiders. When we think about finding our place in the world, though, we may confront additional challenges. If we got our identity from being outsiders, the idea of joining anything can seem a little fishy. Coming back to society is a difficult step, and there may be risk involved. No one can make that decision for us. "I always felt like an outsider when I was growing up. I found acceptance in drug culture," a member shared. That feeling of belonging can be a powerful draw for us; the lifestyle is sometimes harder to let go of than the drugs.

When we take a look at what compels us to put so much emphasis on things outside ourselves, we often find that what is driving us is fear. We are afraid of ourselves, afraid of the world, and afraid someone will find out how afraid we are. We hide behind all sorts of screens, from rigid social conformity to outright hostility. For people who have been through so much, we can be extraordinarily sensitive. We mistakenly believe that social acceptability can give us immunity from the pain that seems to come with caring about what other people think.

Figuring out our strengths and weaknesses can be tricky; sometimes they look a lot alike. All of us are missing pieces and parts. Some of us have a long way to go just to learn the most basic principles of appropriate behavior, while others have mastered the art of covering whatever might be wrong with a coat of lipstick or leather. We can get caught up in looking good, or projecting an image of who we wish we were. If we allow things outside ourselves to define who we are, we end up like a tree with no roots. At the first storm we are liable to come crashing down. When seeking approval becomes more important than recovery, we are more vulnerable to relapse than we recognize.

Getting the outsides right is not only about wanting approval, though. We are learning to respond appropriately to life. Many of us mask low self-esteem with inappropriate behavior. Often we assume that other people will do what we did in our worst moments. We push people away for fear they will see us as we see ourselves. Allowing ourselves to appear in the world as we are is a big step. We are mindful of our behavior and our surroundings without giving up our individuality. But we also begin to let our guard down, let people in, and share who we are. What we find, of course, is that when we are less afraid we tend to be less frightening to others. Ultimately, the issue isn't how society accepts us, but whether we accept society and our role in it.

Our priorities change over the course of our recovery. In the beginning, simply not using is a full-time job. When we transition out of this desperation, many of us get preoccupied with material things. We mistake success for security. When our priorities shift again, it may be a result of a different kind of change: a gradual realization that a deeper satisfaction awaits us. "I believed I was acceptable as long as the bills were paid. I worked hard, but forgot to take care of myself physically, mentally, and spiritually. Gradually, my understanding began to develop. As the connection to my Higher Power deepened, I came to a clearer vision of what I wanted. I was no longer willing to let labels hold me back or define me. I stopped thinking about social acceptability in terms of status. I wanted to be a person people were comfortable being around. After finding my way to the surface and taking that breath of life, I wanted to share it freely, with no false motives."

Finding Our Place in the World

We start with the goal of not using, and our dreams and goals grow as we recover. While some of us crave material success or social status, others want no part of that. Ultimately we define social acceptability for ourselves. Even so, it's a moving target and it changes over time. What we consider an acceptable life in early recovery may seem inadequate or even embarrassing later on. "Just being able to bathe and get through the day without a felony was a big deal for me," said one member. However much or little we have, our feelings of fear or comfort, security or scarcity have more to do with our perspective than anything else. We always remember that a day clean is a day won, no matter how far we have come or how far we have yet to go.

Dreams really do come true, but that's almost never the end of the story. Achievement takes us out past where our planning or projecting ends. We can mistake a goal for an ultimatum: There's only one way it's supposed to be, and anything else is failure. We need to remember that we have only a fleeting glimpse of our Higher Power's will for us. Our desires may set us in a direction, but the journey takes us somewhere that never occurred to us.

Some of us are naturally dynamic and thrive on a lot of color and excitement. We might worry that life we are comfortable with might not be very exciting. Letting go of our attachment to drama makes it possible to enjoy simple things without feeling we must constantly make something happen. We discover that we can be passionate about our lives as they really are. We learn that the kind of work required to live a good life is not nearly as difficult as the kind of work that results from sabotaging our own efforts.

We spent years creating wreckage, damage, and drama; and then cleaning it up to make room for more. When we are spinning our wheels in chaos of our own making, our sponsor might ask us, "What are you running from?" After we stop this destructive cycle, we can see how much it requires of us. We find that we can be radiant without being radioactive. When we're finally able to settle down and breathe, our lives get much easier. That space gives us room to look around and ask ourselves what we love about our lives, and what we might want to change.

Part of what shifts for us is our perception of what constitutes a crisis. Many of us spend much of our early recovery on "high alert." We are so much more aware of the wreckage of our past than the miracle of our recovery that we seem to be in a chronic state of emergency. Addicts are funny: We tend to get very dramatic about little things, but we deal with catastrophe better than most people do. We come to understand more about the scale of our experiences as we live life on life's terms. Experience gives us the ability to put events and situations into proper perspective.

The fewer secrets we have, the less we tend to be concerned about what others are saying or doing. It's our secrets we are afraid of. We hide because we are ashamed. Telling the truth without embellishment or judgment limits drama. Our own willingness to meet the truth and deal with it takes a lot of the air out of the drama in our own minds—and on the gossip circuit. Ongoing step work takes the denial and deception out of our actions. As we learn compassion, we get less pleasure from magnifying the struggles of others.

When we work hard and earn a victory, we certainly can be proud of ourselves. However, there is a big difference between feeling good about ourselves and believing our own hype. We are in trouble when we start mistaking outside success for recovery. When we allow our humility and integrity to decay, we are a danger to ourselves and everyone around us. If we confuse our priorities, we can lose more than we thought we had at stake. And when we try to fill up the empty places inside us with material things or lofty positions, we find that we are emptier than before. When our gratitude is gone, we forget where we came from and no longer relate to the newcomer. We are so lost in delusion that we don't even know there is a problem. Many members have died as a result of such arrogance. Net worth does not equal self-worth. We have all seen members achieve great success and still use or want to destroy themselves.

Perhaps because we have been so far outside society, we tend to be very conscious of how it works. Addicts seem to have a nose for deceit. We have no time for people playing fast and loose with the truth, even if we struggle to consistently practice honesty ourselves. It's our own struggle with honesty that makes the principle so important to us. We know how easy it is to let go of our integrity in favor of short-term gain, even when we know the consequences. We are acutely insightful about relationships between people and about the flow of money and power, and we know how to position ourselves to get what we want. So it's no surprise that so many of us get caught up in chasing status, either inside or outside the fellowship.

We find freedom when we learn to be ourselves and support our own efforts. This is not just a financial issue. When we apply the Seventh Tradition to our own lives, we discover that we have some pretty twisted ideas about independence. On one hand, we may be fiercely aloof, unwilling to trust others or to risk getting too attached to anyone or anything. On the other hand, we may be accustomed to getting our needs met without having to take responsibility. Some of us feared independence in our active addiction, clinging to our partners or families for support. Being institutionalized led some of us to feel absolutely alone, but without any autonomy at all. "Getting out of prison was freedom," said one member, "but it was also terrifying. I didn't know how to live, and I wasn't too sure I wanted to learn." Learning to make decisions for ourselves also means accepting responsibility for those decisions.

Blaming others and harboring resentments can be a way to pretend we have no responsibility for the work we must do inside ourselves and out in the world. "I went to jail clean," said a member. "I kept feeding my disease without drugs until I learned to apply the program to all areas of my life. Step Four began the demolition process that prepared me for society. I had to learn how to participate without being destructive." Taking responsibility for ourselves is necessary for us to move forward, and it opens the door to the amends process. It is an amends to those who care for us that we are no longer a burden on them. It is an amends to society that we can give back. And it is an amends to ourselves when we practice self-determination, making our own way and our own choices.

One of the benefits of taking a personal inventory is that we don't have to wait for someone else to tell us who we are or how we are. When we are willing to stand for our own dreams and beliefs, we are practicing a deeper kind of self-support. We develop the ability to choose what is right for us and to stand for it even when it's not what others believe. We don't have to be defensive to stand up for ourselves and our principles. With new perspective, we start to trust our recovery and our instincts. Addicts have really good instincts—and really bad impulses. Learning to recognize the difference takes time and practice. A sponsor and trusted friends can help us sort out the difference between our desires and our compulsions.

We may change because we choose to, or change may happen as a result of circumstances beyond our control. Our lives require ongoing maintenance, and our definitions of success change as life gives and takes. "I had success in all areas of my life. After a change in my career and a move to a new town, it was all gone—my success, self-esteem, even my joy in participation at NA meetings. I was an oldtimer and I didn't know what to do. I began to understand that my recovery and self-worth were based in externals. When success and approval left, I collapsed. A new perspective and a walk through the steps from a different angle were necessary." Comparing our current problems to the problems we had in active addiction can be a tactic we use to avoid dealing with them. We sometimes belittle the struggles we face as "gold-plated problems," but if we ignore them we may get a "gold-plated" relapse. Ultimately, our success is measured not from the outside but from the inside. When we apply the principles in our lives we succeed in many ways, but most of all we become whole.

The idea of integration is closely linked to the spiritual principle of integrity. Integrity is unity within ourselves: We are the same person wherever we are. Our commitment to our values as we understand them is not based on convenience or circumstance. We don't have to pretend to be someone else, or hold one side of ourselves to the light and hide the rest, in order to function or be accepted. Our comfort with ourselves is attractive. When we are practicing integrity, we can walk with dignity whether or not we find approval outside ourselves: We know who we are.

Freedom comes from discovering who we are inside. Recovering addicts are brilliant, creative, and compassionate people, whether we know it about ourselves or not. The steps help us to develop integrity, a realistic perspective on ourselves, a means to achieve self-acceptance, and a process to become acceptable to society. Many of us don't feel like we are good enough for life in recovery, and we show it in the way we treat ourselves. When we practice respect and compassion for ourselves, our thoughts and feelings start to change. Self-acceptance frees us to take responsibility for our lives and to accept the gifts that are available to us. When we take the Serenity Prayer seriously and really consider what in our lives we do have the courage to change, we find that our ability to shape our lives is limited more by our willingness than by anything outside ourselves.

Stability

Like so many things we strive for in recovery, stability is an inside job. The feeling of stability starts from the knowledge that we are okay no matter what happens. It's a sense of security and safety in our own lives. We may believe that this will be a result of achieving goals—like getting a house, a partner, a job, or some imagined amount of money. But when fear grips us, it doesn't matter what we have or who we share it with. The security that we seek comes from peace within ourselves, a relationship with a Higher Power, and connection with others. Coming to believe that our life is really ours can take a long time.

For some of us, stability begins when we are willing to commit to a fixed address. We may begin with regular attendance at a home group and work our way up from there. Others of us come in with all the trappings of a normal life, but find that "trappings" are exactly what they are. We may need to break free from the ties that bind us to our old lives before we can be ourselves. Security, predictability, and a feeling of belonging allow us to change without feeling like we're losing ourselves. A member shared: "When I was using, I always had a change of clothes in my purse because I never knew where I would wake up. After I got clean I started picking up more and more furniture until my house was overflowing. Later I realized I was taking on all this stuff to make sure it was hard to move. I didn't really want more dishes; what I wanted was to know I was going to be somewhere for a while." Serenity may be the presence of peace or the absence of chaos.

Many of us have gone through life by default, as if events simply happened to us. Our sense of ourselves was so distorted that we felt like we had no impact on the world. When we understand the First Step, we realize that "I'm powerless over everything" is a cop-out. We are powerless over our addiction, and we cannot turn back time. Beyond that, we may be amazed at the ability we have to make choices and shape our lives. Our relationship with the world is a reflection of our relationship with ourselves. We are open to new ideas, new ways of thinking, and new ways of seeing what we think we know. Trusting people who believe in us allows us to try new things even when they seem frightening, and to have faith that the changes we see are real.

Our sense of stability within ourselves allows us to take greater risks, whether that means being willing to pursue a new career or to put our hearts on the line with someone we love. When we learn to trust that stability, we can let go a little more. We no longer spend our days or nights worrying—or wishing—that it will all go away. "I'm so afraid to show up and grow up that I dream of running away, starting over, leaving it all behind." We fear security because we don't quite trust that we are capable of sustaining it. Staying with the process of our lives without creating upheaval and drama can be a new experience for us.

Stability is important for us to thrive, but there is a difference between being stable and being stuck. It may be that we stop moving forward because we have arrived at a destination. Of course we want to enjoy the fruits of our labor, but we run the risk of enjoying that fruit until it rots. "When I got clean it was relatively easy for me to make the transition to a normal lifestyle," said one member. "But fear of change kept me paralyzed there." We have a hard time distinguishing between a niche and a ditch.

There are some signs that help us to distinguish serenity from complacency: When we get judgmental, ungrateful, and agitated, we're probably on the wrong side of that line. When interacting with others starts to seem exhausting or burdensome, or we forget that we are important to others, we might be slipping back into self-obsession. When we're feeling apathetic and ungrateful, we say we're "bored."

Boredom usually means we can't see past ourselves. We get lost in pettiness and illusion. The world is as boring or exciting as we make it. A member shared, "When one day starts to run into another, it's usually because I'm not living my beliefs." When we revert to old behavior, we need to get back to basics. Cleantime does not exempt us from getting stuck. Sometimes a new perspective on our lives requires a new look at the steps. We may find that a better attitude is really all we need—or it may be time to make some changes in our lives.

We are able to recognize our responsibility for our actions and motives more often, and sooner in the process. Identifying what drives us helps us to find relief from all the ways the disease shows up in our lives. It also gives us the ability to move toward what we want, and not just away from what we fear.

We are free to create a life that we value. When we are collaborating with our Higher Power, action and surrender go hand in hand. We can spend a lot of time trying to convince our Higher Power how things should go. Each of us has had the experience of trying to will something into being and finding that the most bizarre obstacles arise until we finally understand that the best thing we can do is to let go. On the other hand, sometimes a challenge or commitment just keeps placing itself before us. No matter how hard we try not to do it, it seems unavoidable. When we surrender and try, we are astounded at what we can accomplish. The more completely we surrender, the more we are able to follow through on our commitments and shine.

Getting Out of Our Own Way

So much of our experience is a result of our perception. We may feel very grounded even though the outside circumstances of our lives are in flux. There are also times when everything looks fine, but we feel like we're coming undone. We can come through letdowns and redirections and see that we are still succeeding and progressing in our lives. Or we can feel like a failure even when everything is actually going along just fine. Perhaps what we perceive as good or bad is simply an event. We make it good or bad by our attitude toward it and our response to it. We can turn a simple setback into a drama that lasts forever and is everyone else's fault. We get through difficulty much more quickly if we simply accept it and keep moving. Letting go gets easier when we learn not to hold on so tightly.

It may be that the sky is not the limit for us. There may be limitations set by our lives or circumstances that make some of our choices for us. More often, we are held back by barriers we put in our own way. We get so accustomed to thinking of ourselves in particular ways that it's hard to imagine otherwise. We can be brutal to ourselves. Giving ourselves a break is one of the most important skills we gain in recovery, and it is critical to our ability to change. It's hard to learn something new if we can't allow ourselves to be imperfect. Our shortcomings and defects keep us from being able to act in our own best interest. Some of the hardest things to get free of may be our own beliefs about ourselves and our limitations.

Obstacles give us a chance to examine our willingness. Some of us fight our way to a goal despite physical disabilities, criminal records, or other hurdles. The obstacles in our path can make us more committed to our goals. We find a way to do the impossible. At other times, barriers drive us to think creatively and to look in other directions for where we can best use our energies.

How often we succeed or fail is not the measure of our program. Our setbacks don't have the power to define us. Failure is experience, strength, and hope in disguise. It is incredibly important to learn the difference between failing at something and "being a failure." When we are honest, we begin to take responsibility for our part. Remorse can fuel a new willingness to change. Failure, just like success, has an important role to play in our lives, taking us places we would never choose to go. It can free us to pursue new things, and to seek even broader horizons.

Sometimes what we experience as failure is actually a redirection. We can get so focused that it takes a serious push to change our course. After getting through a hard time clean, a member said: "I needed to fail. I was completely out of control because I thought I was completely in control. I had confused outside success with internal growth in recovery." We respond to our own fear by getting more controlling, and create more problems as a result. Often when we are deeply challenged in one area of our lives, other areas start to suffer. When things get difficult, it never seems like just one thing goes wrong. We start using old behaviors again, even though we know—or we once knew—that they don't work. Unmanageability feeds on itself. A hard lesson in humility reminds us that we never graduate. When we stop practicing the basics, we are in trouble.

It takes courage to put ourselves on the line. If the risks we are taking are real, then certainly sometimes we will lose. If we don't occasionally fall short, it probably means we are setting the bar too low. We learn through our mistakes, and the experience can strengthen our faith and resolve. Most importantly, we don't have to do it alone. As we accept that we will be okay even when we are disappointed, we start to feel a little more comfortable with the idea of taking risks. We learn to listen to our instincts and start to move with the rhythm of our lives. We can respond to changes as they happen without being distracted by our desire to judge or explain them.

We set goals for ourselves and move toward them a day at a time, an inch at a time, knowing that when we're doing the right things, the right things tend to happen—even if they're not what we anticipate. We have a tendency to act as if our progress doesn't count until we have arrived at our goals. Learning to keep going through setbacks or hard times allows us to continue moving forward even when things are not going our way.

Some of us never get where we meant to go, and it does not mean there is anything wrong with our recovery. We are not staying clean for the rewards; though staying clean can be very rewarding. Whatever gifts we do or do not receive, we do well to remember that there is nothing wrong today that a case of withdrawal won't make worse. We all experience loss and hardship at some point in our recovery, and if we are not willing to accept that as part of the process, our desire for success can turn insidiously into a reservation. If we are ashamed by the difficulty we are going through or feel that we cannot be honest about our struggles, our relationship to the fellowship will suffer no matter how much cleantime we have.

Many of us have expectations that if we do our recovery right, there will be no difficulty or pain and we will get everything that we want. These expectations can be lethal. We may want to believe that if we work a good enough program we won't ever lose, when in fact working a program helps us keep going no matter what. Some of us experience only small losses, while others endure tragedy—sometimes over and over. Moving forward isn't easy, but it's what we do. We can't set limits or time frames around our feelings. "I needed to be brutally honest about how I felt," said a member, "even when it made my stomach hurt. I was sad, angry, afraid, and jealous of others who had already succeeded." We don't need to be told how to experience our feelings, but it's nice to know we are loved and supported through them. Once we go through a hard time clean, we know we can get through difficulty and be all right. We start to believe in our own resilience and to trust our recovery. We find faith and strength inside ourselves that cannot be taken away unless we give it away.

If we have a history of failure, it may be hard for us to believe that success is a possibility. Our past experience may not always be a good guide. Just as the Second Step taught us that insanity is doing the same things and expecting different results, sometimes we do different things and expect the same results. Even though we are not doing what we always did, we still expect to get what we always got. We learn that things really can change for us, if we are willing. If we want something we never had, we will need to try some things we have never tried, and have some faith.

When we change our actions, beliefs, and motives, our lives change—but not always the way we think they will. The open-mindedness we practice in our recovery gives us the ability to be flexible when things change in ways we hadn't expected. "I've learned to be open-minded about all kinds of things," said a member, "including what makes me happy." We may be free a long time before we recognize it.

We are careful not to hold one another back or discourage one another from trying to follow our dreams. "After many years of sponsorship," one member said, "I finally realized I wasn't going to keep anyone from doing what they really wanted to do. The question was whether they were going to be comfortable sharing honestly with me about it. When I set demands or limitations, I became one more thing for my sponsees to work around." We help each other to see clearly what we may be getting ourselves into, but we also listen for our own guidance.

The real issue may not be our ultimate failure or success, but our faith in the process. Another addict shared: "I had years clean when everything fell apart: marriage, job, finances, and my relationship with my kids. People reminded me that every clean day was a successful day. That didn't seem good enough anymore. I thought they were putting me down. But I actually was successfully working an NA program. I needed a priority adjustment. I'm still putting things back together, but today I am happier and more fulfilled." We start to see that big changes in our lives are not the end of the world, just the end of a phase or an experiment. A member observed, "I thought 'no matter what' meant don't use even if there's an earthquake. But I am learning it also means keep going even when you don't feel like it."

Continuing to do as we were taught even when the sky is falling doesn't just get us through. When we experience hardship, we can get angry and resistant. It can be hard to sit through a meeting or hear what anyone else has to say. We think we can just put our heads down and bull through it, but that tends to make things worse. It's like saying, "I'm just going to run on my own will until I get through this hard time, then I'll turn it back over." When we keep coming to meetings even with our attitude, we hear the message in spite of ourselves. We show up, and the message finds us whether we are looking for it or not. We learn from the experience and we grow. We often find that the new place we are in as a result is better than what we had resisted letting go.

A Leap of Faith

NA gives us different versions of success and failure than the rest of the world. Our lives are successful because we are clean, we help people, and we have a relationship with a power greater than ourselves. That can be hard to remember when our outsides are in turmoil. If life is a dream, then we may occasionally have nightmares! We experience ups and downs, but we have a disease that tells us it was "always like this," however well or poorly we're doing. We can get drawn into thinking either that we're immune to failure or that life will always be difficult for us. We each go through hard times and great success, and we learn that they are not the whole story—or even the most important part of the story.

Both success and failure can be challenging for us. Some of us create crisis because we don't know how to deal with positive experiences. We may fear success because it will bring more responsibility, and that feels like a trap. We may be concerned that success will lead us to lose focus on staying clean. It may simply be that avoiding a challenge is easier than risking failure. Perhaps we don't feel worthy, or failing feels normal.

Recovery is a process of evolution. We want to become the best person we can, doing work we feel is important, feeling loved and valued. There cannot be only one way to do that, because we are all different. We want to be given a road map to success, but few of us find that kind of specific direction gets us very far. We learn what is right for us through our own efforts.

We may not have dreams when we get here. Our experience may have taught us that it's not safe to share our dreams or to want them too much. We have to find a way to hear our own desires. Over time, we gain a keener understanding of what it means to live in harmony with our beliefs. Even when we share our lives with others, our willingness to fulfill our responsibility to ourselves determines our ability to feel love and be satisfied with our lives. It's the integrity with which we live our lives that is important. After all, if we don't like who we are or how we act, if we find our own company uncomfortable, does it really matter what or how much we have?

We build a foundation, a fellowship, and a life—not necessarily in that order. Those of us who have been fortunate enough to be involved in developing an NA community know how gratifying it is to grow something from a seed. The experience is unlike anything we know. Many of us devote ourselves heart and soul to NA, and the process of building our own lives comes later. We may find ourselves beginning a career or to seeing to our financial security years after our peers seem very settled. There is no right or wrong way or order in which our recovery happens.

We all have experience starting over in our lives with new people, places, and things, stepping into a new way of life we don't quite understand. The desire to survive and feel fulfilled is not unique to us as addicts. In recovery, we begin with connection to others and work our way to basic safety. And perhaps it has to be this way. To believe that we can trust the love in our lives is challenging. Those really deep needs are the ones we believe won't be met. It begins with the amends process: the understanding that we can forgive and be forgiven, that we can take responsibility for our actions and make better choices.

Throughout our recovery we improve our behavior, our attitudes, our perspectives, and our lives. The awakenings we have as we work the first eleven steps give us the ability to act in a new way. We ask for knowledge of our Higher Power's will for us *and the power* to carry that out. After all the surrendering and housecleaning in the previous steps, a constant conscious contact in the Eleventh Step changes us. The more we embrace our powerlessness, the more deeply empowered we are to take action in our lives. Our Basic Text tells us that we find God's will for us in the things we value the most. We may describe this in very spiritual language, or just know the feeling of being at one with what we are doing. "I know I'm doing my Higher Power's will when all that noise in my head goes away."

On some level, this is all about faith. Living our dreams requires that we believe they are possible. When we act on faith, we move in a positive direction. It can be very frightening and sometimes a little weird. Taking a leap of faith asks us to trust either that there will be ground beneath our feet or that we will be able to fly. Small steps give us the courage to leap.

Commitment

The tools we use to practice our recovery serve us in all our affairs. Imagination is a tool, and when we give ourselves permission to dream we are using that tool to explore our own hearts. It can be frightening to look at what we really believe, what we want, and who we are. By practicing prayer and meditation, we learn to listen to our own inner voice and to know when something is true for us. The people we trust help us to sort out the truth within us from the driving voice of compulsion. We make decisions born of desire—just like staying clean. "We tell newcomers to suit up, show up, and give NA everything they've got. Why shouldn't I do this in other areas of my life?" a member asked. Learning to dream is important, but it's not a way of life. Willingness without action is fantasy.

It's one thing to have faith in a power greater than ourselves, and quite another to have faith in ourselves. Some of us take a long time to come to believe that we can contribute to the world in a way that serves a greater good, or that serves our values and sense of purpose. Doing the right thing when no one is looking is an act of service to what we believe in. Some of us call this integrity; the Sixth Step calls it character. Whatever we call it, this practice is the discipline that forms the basis of our growing maturity.

As principles go, discipline might be one of the less popular. We talk about commitment almost from our first day clean. We make a commitment to show up, to stay clean until our next meeting, to call someone before we pick up. Acting on the commitments we make requires discipline, and that's a skill we develop as we practice. It doesn't come naturally to most of us, but our long-term goals are often served by postponing short-term gratification. Discipline is commitment in action, a demonstration of our willingness. It is different from "willpower" or "self-will" in that we are not trying to force ourselves to change. We are changing our relationship to our own behavior. The more we trust the process, the more we are willing to practice discipline. "I got where I am by the grace of God—and a stubborn refusal to go away," a member shared. When discipline and faith come together, we begin to become the people we wished we could be.

Talent or interest may come naturally, but any skill takes practice. Developing the focus and energy to stay on task is one challenge; allowing ourselves to take risks is another. It takes courage to face our own creativity and discipline it to produce the things we want. A member shared: "I don't feel I have the freedom on the inside to do what I have the ability to do on the outside. I see that as a future freedom."

Awareness is not the same as control. We don't automatically get freedom from our defects just because we see them. Awareness gives us hope and direction. Sometimes that can be a motivator to get us working, and sometimes the best we can do is wait. When we can't see our way around a defect or an obstacle, it's often because there is other work that must be done first. Self-acceptance frees our imagination. Work on the amends steps allows us to feel worthy of success. The answers are in different places for each of us, and we may not know them until we've found them. Doing the work of recovery frees us in ways we can't predict. It's only in experiencing freedom that we learn we were bound before.

Goals are dreams we put into action. We can understand the work and measure our progress more easily if we break our goals down into steps. After all, we know a thing or two about doing things in steps! Setting achievable goals and celebrating milestones along the way allows us to see our progress, and gives us moments when we can step back and evaluate where we are and where we are going.

Education

Addiction can be pretty disruptive to education. Some of us stopped early in the process, or never felt engaged by it at all. There are gaps in our knowledge, either as a result of our addiction or where we come from, and these can be a source of shame as well. Lack of information is not a character defect; it's just something we don't know yet. There is a difference between not knowing and not being teachable.

Recovery is an education. We are learning principles and practicing a new way of life. In the process, we learn to read, write, care, share, practice, show up, and keep coming back. The abilities we develop as we work the steps are easily transferable. When we apply these skills to other kinds of learning, we tend to do surprisingly well, even though the method may be very different. Even if we are starting at the beginning, there are few limits to how far we can go.

Many of us go back to school after we get clean, and we can be surprised at the challenges we confront. Even a training program at work can be intimidating when we are not used to learning that way. It's not something all of us do, and many of us go back for a little while and decide it's not for us. "I was grateful for the opportunity, but I also found out I didn't have to do that," said a member. We may go back to school because we need new skills, or just because we want to try something new. "I had really distorted ideas about what society was," said one member, "and what the playing field was. Before I could fully participate, I had to learn how it worked."

We learn more than just the subject we are studying. We learn how to learn. Just as our bodies were damaged by our addiction, our brains have taken a beating. Whatever we study, whether it's playing the guitar, welding, knitting, or philosophy, learning gives our minds a workout. We can see and feel the healing as we practice absorbing and retaining information. We learn to work under pressure and to accept feedback. We learn to persevere through a learning curve. Impatience is a stumbling block: We want to know something, not to learn it. Studying is an exercise in staying focused. Our practice at being teachable is a good start.

Some of us go back to school with a specific plan in mind, but we can surprise ourselves. The joy of learning can be its own reward. We may not know what we are good at, and chances are we're smarter than we think. "I believed I was stupid because it took me so many years of relapsing to get clean," a member shared. "Getting a degree helped me to believe in my own intelligence." Being open-minded about our talents can allow us to follow a path we had not imagined.

Many of us share the feeling that we must catch up or make up for the time lost to our addiction. We struggle with the feeling that we are somehow just not enough. Making time for our commitments at school and in NA can be a lesson in balance. We may imagine that all of our classmates are using, or that "they" are a unit we don't fit into. We can be insecure and judgmental at the same time. "The process was surprisingly emotional," shared a member. "I wore my recovery like armor. I felt lonely and unnoticed, but I didn't have the self-acceptance to let anyone in."

If we tend toward perfectionism at all, chances are we'll get to confront it when we go to school. A member shared: "I felt like a failure if I got less than a perfect score on a test. I couldn't sleep until I figured out where I had gone wrong. I wasn't competing against the other students: I was competing against my own fear." Right behind perfectionism is a wall of shame. Any misstep feels like it opens a window on that secret. Suggestions feel like criticism, and criticism feels like condemnation.

Often we act as if our lives will really begin at some future time: When we get a certain amount of cleantime, when we finish school, when we get that job, or when our lives have magically become manageable. In a "just for today" program, we learn that what matters is not what will happen at a future date. Our lives are what we're doing right now. The way we live on the way to our goals is the way we live. Tall trees require deep roots. We need to ensure that we are taking the time to build and maintain our foundation as we move forward.

Money

Whether we have a lot of it or very little, most of us have a challenging relationship to money. There is no one right set of values, but we do have principles that we practice. Our Seventh Tradition talks about being self-supporting through our own contributions, and while the tradition makes direct reference to the groups, many of us find that practicing the principle in our own lives is essential to experiencing freedom. We learn to support ourselves financially, and we find that there are other ways in which we can practice self-support. We learn to carry our own weight, clean up our own mess, and contribute in the places that are important to us. It can be very hard for us to share about our relationship to money. Sharing honestly about this with our sponsor can open the door to healing in all areas of our lives.

Having money and working may be totally unrelated when we get here. We found the financial resources that we needed in our active addiction in all sorts of other ways. We stole, we manipulated, we took advantage, we persuaded others of our entitlement. We were takers, and we squandered the resources that were made available to us. In our self-centeredness we were oblivious to the toll we took on the people around us. The awareness that we might never be able to repay what we owe can be part of the force that drives us to a new way of life. We owe a debt, and every time we act in the service of a greater good we can feel something shifting inside us. We have a contribution to make, and making it is not a sacrifice: It serves us at least as much as those we serve.

The sense of entitlement that enabled us to live as we did in our addiction can follow us into recovery. Often it shows up in more subtle forms. We don't steal people's purses anymore, but it may seem perfectly reasonable to take supplies from work, to shoplift a little, to continue taking advantage of people. We may know that this kind of dishonesty is wrong, but harbor the sense that we're not being paid what we're worth, that we deserve a break we're not getting, or that the people we serve at work, at home, or in NA should be more grateful than they are. Sometimes it shows up in our distrust of others: We constantly suspect that someone is trying to get over on us.

This simmering resentment can be incredibly destructive. We see not what we have but what we lack. We feel our vulnerability rather than our security. It's hard to be happy when the world feels like a hostile place. Learning to practice faith and gratitude does not mean that we give up our "street smarts." It means we start to develop a different kind of intelligence. We can stand up for ourselves without feeling like we are fighting for our lives. We begin to trust that our needs will be met, and to see the imperfections in our circumstances as opportunities rather than barriers to growth.

Even in recovery, obsession and compulsion play out in our spending habits. We shop impulsively or compulsively, and get obsessed with having the newest or the best. We use our money unwisely in an attempt to fill the void: We want to buy love, approval, or the appearance of success. "I thought I could buy my way out of addiction," said one member. Money becomes one more way to play out our control issues, and we get so rigid that we create more problems than we solve. Or we simply let money and opportunities go by, feeling like poverty is probably appropriate for us. Some of us find that it's not "stuff" that attracts us, but the pursuit. This drive can bring us to great success or it can be the compulsion that fuels yet another symptom of our addiction. We are the only ones who really know the truth. If we are gambling, working the system, opening and closing businesses, veering from financial success to failure and back again, we might want to take a look at what we're up to. It can be difficult to admit that we have a troubled relationship with money; sharing honestly with someone we trust can begin the process of change. Financial unmanageability is often a symptom of a larger issue. Like so many things we struggle with, it is a practical problem with a spiritual solution.

"Very small things," one member shared, "like paying the bills on time, gave me a feeling of self-worth." Another member shared that she began to overcome her resentment of paying her bills by writing "Thank you for your services" on her payments. Simply meeting our own obligations can be a victory. For some of us, this resolves quickly. Others spend a lifetime learning to manage. Financial turmoil is not unusual for NA members, but it is not a requirement. Acting out on our disease has financial consequences. But many of the ways we show our recovery have financial consequences, too. This doesn't mean that when we are working our program we get rich. Some of us never make as much money in recovery as we did when we were using, and being responsible can be expensive. But many of us find success in recovery, and do achieve financial comfort. When we are practicing sanity and living within our means, we can be comfortable with ourselves and our circumstances, no matter what they are.

We also learn to ask for help when we need it. Many of us struggle in recovery when we become sick or disabled because our beliefs about being self-supporting make it hard to seek the assistance we may desperately need. The humility we learn from working the steps allows us to ask for help when necessary, and to know that we are neither too good to have needs nor too bad to deserve a hand. We may find that what we want is very different from what we need, and learning to adapt to our circumstances can give us a flexibility that we hadn't imagined before. We learn to accept help, and find other ways to contribute as well. Losing everything isn't a life sentence, just as having it all doesn't mean we will not be in need again.

Prudence is a principle some of us practice more than others. It's a funny word, but it's what we are talking about when we refer in service to a "prudent reserve." A member shared: "I learned to be responsible and prudent with NA funds, so I don't misappropriate other people's funds either. I have learned the principles of honesty and accountability. It's part of walking my talk and applying the principles."

In service, we learn to take on obligations thoughtfully to ensure that we can follow through on what we've promised. In other areas of our lives as well, we find that planning and following through makes us feel good about ourselves. We do our best to ensure that we can be responsible even if our circumstances change. "I went through a hard time in my business and had to live off my savings for a while. I was ashamed to talk about it in meetings, but I shared with a fellow addict. Later he told me that this was a message of hope for him. Because I planned ahead, I was able to make it through a tough time. What I saw as a failure, he saw as a success. One more time, I gained a better perspective on my life."

We also notice in NA that those who do not give it away tend not to keep it; the idea that giving is a crucial part of having is something many of us are surprised to discover. We may or may not have material wealth, but our emotional, spiritual, and mental resources are enormous. We have a wealth of experience. When we give our energy, time, talent, and creativity, we are rewarded many times over.

Work

While the steps help us to become better people, service is one way we learn how to function in the world again. Many of the skills we learn in service translate into our working lives. We may sometimes feel like outsiders or imposters in our jobs, but in NA service we are full participants. We don't second-guess our primary purpose or our right to participate. In a fellowship where the ultimate authority is a power greater than ourselves, we learn how to work with others as a peer with something to offer and something to learn, rather than seeing ourselves as an authority or a victim. We learn to channel our energy in a constructive direction, and we can practice staying focused. We stretch beyond our current abilities and find that we can survive and succeed even if we are not perfect. Service counteracts selfishness and increases our feelings of self-worth. We learn to step back and think before we respond. Not everything that affects us is personal, and we don't have to return fire every time. NA gives us a safe place to make mistakes, find out who we are, and learn how to relate to people. The things that make us defensive or self-righteous tend to be pretty much the same wherever we go. We see our character defects manifesting and find humility, make amends, or just change course and start over. Everyone makes mistakes; promptly admitting when we are wrong shows integrity and responsibility for our actions.

The experience of service helps us take on responsibilities and learn to meet them as we go. We learn to sit still and listen, and to make our voice heard when we have something to say. We start to feel we can take our rightful place in the world, without feeling fear or shame. As we practice these principles in all our affairs, some of the distinctions between who we are in our work lives and in our recovery lives begin to fall away.

One way we practice these principles is to be of service to our employer. Some members have asked themselves: "How do I practice unity at work? How do I let my HP be in charge during my workday? What is the primary purpose of this workplace, and how can I help achieve that? What is my primary purpose here?" Whatever our job is, when we can see it as an opportunity to practice our principles it becomes a worthy use of our time. A member shared: "Responsibility used to feel like a burden to me. Learning to see it as a way to do my Higher Power's will made it feel like a privilege." With spiritual principles as our guide, we can be an asset wherever we are. Often the people around us see our value before we do. Perhaps most of all, when we are spiritually connected, creativity flows through us. This doesn't necessarily mean that we paint or make music (though it can), but that we can see solutions to problems and find satisfaction in doing whatever we do as best we can.

The transition from NA to work is not always seamless. We may be really shocked to find that outside NA the Third Tradition does not apply. We are not members of other groups just because we want to be. We may have to earn our seat at another table, and there are some places we may never be accepted as we would wish. Additionally, what would seem perfectly natural with our NA friends can be inappropriate or even shocking elsewhere. We are conscious of how we share our feelings and our histories. We learn the difference between friendships, recovery relationships, and professional relationships, and we begin to understand that we can alter our behavior without having to compromise ourselves.

As we advance in our step work, we are more capable of acknowledging our progress in other areas as well. The humility that we learn in the steps helps us find where we belong in the world. We start to feel that we are no better or worse than anyone else, even at work, and that our gifts are useful. One member talked about finding a job that suited his "skills and ills"; when we find the right environment, we see that we can be distinguished by some of the things that used to make us most uncomfortable about ourselves. Some of us are naturally industrious, and others are really good at sitting still and being present in the moment. Either one can be an asset or a defect, depending on how we use it. The guilt of being unproductive and stealing time at work feeds on itself. On the other hand, the drive to stay in constant motion can be a consequence of fear. When we don't take time to reflect on what we're doing and how we're doing it, small mistakes can add up quickly. As with everything else we do, we seek a healthy balance.

Our issues may differ, but the principles we practice are the same. Some of us never worked before we got clean, and for others of us work was all we did. By the same token, some of us don't need to work for financial reasons, and some are too disabled to be able to work steadily anymore. Still, we can benefit from keeping a schedule and being accountable. We may resist structure in our lives, but it can help us enormously. We are, after all, creatures of habit. When we feel we have a purpose that gives shape to our days, we are more comfortable with ourselves and our lives. Our work can be something we do to fill time or to pay the bills, or it may be one of the primary ways we define ourselves. Those of us who have work that is meaningful or valuable to us are fortunate. It's a goal many of us work toward, and when we feel that we're doing a good job at something that matters, it brings a deep satisfaction. Whoever we are, wherever we come from, we have something to offer.

Our work ethic is the collection of habits that determine how we use our time. When we set our minds to something, we can be exceptionally determined. Few people are ever as driven in their lives as an addict in search of a fix. When we learn to turn that determination toward healthy goals, we can achieve amazing things. We know if we do something regularly, it will become a habit for us. What begins as discipline develops into habit, and eventually it becomes a pleasure. There is danger in this method, however. Substitution can be deadly, especially when it seems to be working for us. The hallmark of our disease is progression. When we notice that our relationship to an activity has allowed us to justify unmanageability elsewhere in our lives, it's probably time for a good, hard look at our actions, our motives—and our steps.

We can be haunted by feelings of inadequacy well into our recovery, and spend our time and energy trying to prove ourselves or live up to an unattainable and imaginary standard. We may swing between being very insecure and eager to please, and resisting the most basic rules and requirements of a job. Our lack of self-acceptance shows when we can't take compliments. When we feel bad about ourselves or unworthy, we tend to overcompensate. We may find ourselves covering for others or taking undesirable shifts for fear that we are somehow more expendable than others. "I excelled at work," said a member, "but I still didn't feel responsible or productive. Inadequacy haunted me." It can be hard to tell the difference between a genuine desire to do better and performance that's driven by fear.

When fear is driving us, we may notice that procrastination becomes an issue. We are afraid to finish what we start, and begin making excuses. "When I get close to the end of a project, it feels like I'm in a wind tunnel. I don't know where the resistance comes from, but it's so strong I can barely get my feet under me." We can have so many ideas and so much unfinished business that making a decision about what to do next compounds our anxiety. One addict shared that he "felt like a quarter horse in a one-mile race: a great starter but a really poor finisher."

Sometimes we can even use our defects to our advantage. For example, we may beat ourselves up because we procrastinate what we fear. We can also use that energy to get a lot of other things done. "I am rarely more productive than when I'm procrastinating," said one member. "I might get the whole house clean because I'm putting off studying, or I'll get the bills done because I don't want to have a hard conversation." But all that effort spent on busywork doesn't get us closer to our goal. Sooner or later, we must admit the truth and deal with the thing we are avoiding. Most of the time, the avoidance takes much more energy than the doing. Efficiency is the result of clearing out that defective stuff that drains us of our time and energy.

We strive for balance, and we find it in different ways. When we get more comfortable with ourselves, we are more comfortable with others as well. Our willingness and humility show as a genuine desire to do better, no matter how well we are doing—not because we have something to prove, but because we care. We can practice principles in the workplace without being naïve or overly eager to please. As we stay clean, we develop a new history. Our colleagues may not have seen us in desperation and might have no reason to guess that we are addicts in recovery. We don't have to let go of our anonymity to integrate who we are into our careers. That's a choice we can make for ourselves. We are human beings, doing our best to be responsible and productive.

Working can become an alibi for not practicing our program. We have heard many times that we will lose anything we put in front of our recovery, and many of us have experienced this with jobs or material things that seemed to make recovery obsolete or inconvenient. When we are using the tools available to us, we can see the challenges we encounter in our work as opportunities to practice our program. Applying the principles never makes life worse. When we are not practicing our program, our problems become magnified unreasonably. We feel overly responsible, obsessed, and compelled to keep going, even when a break might be the thing that would give us needed perspective.

We are successful members of society, in and out of the workforce. We have as much integrity toward our jobs and the people we serve outside the rooms as we do inside the rooms—and that's the point. When we practice these principles in all our affairs, we bring so much to the world. It's not just a theory or another awful lecture about our "potential." It's our experience; it's what we do.

Anonymity

Our addiction no longer sets us apart, but making the decision to tell people about our membership in NA should be done with care. We can be recklessly casual about our anonymity. "Anonymous" is half our name for a reason. There is still stigma attached to being an addict, and there may also be consequences to admitting we're in recovery. Caution isn't the only reason for anonymity. The Twelfth Tradition tells us that it is our spiritual foundation. The fact that we are anonymous means that the work we do in NA really can be selfless service. We don't want or need credit for helping others; it's what we do to save our own lives. We don't benefit from sympathy for our condition; the price for that is ultimately too high. In the rooms we are equals with one another, and out of the rooms we are equals with our peers.

We check our motives before we share with someone that we are addicts, and we learn that this is good policy any time we consider disclosing something significant about ourselves. Taking a moment to pray and consider our intentions frees us to use our experience as a tool rather than a weapon. We consider whether we are seeking attention, making ourselves look important, trying to justify our behavior, or whether we are able to offer help or guidance as a result of our experience. We may be letting someone get to know us better, creating a bridge for empathy. We also want to consider our own boundaries: Is this someone we feel safe to share with? Would someone else's anonymity be compromised by our disclosure? Are we limiting or protecting the relationship by not sharing about ourselves? Is our action taking us outside the boundaries set for us by the Eleventh Tradition? We have something to share that has value in and out of the rooms. It is ours, and we have choices about it.

That said, there are times when it is appropriate to let go of our anonymity—and, of course, there are times when people find out through no action of our own. We have choices about how we want to respond. A member shared his experience: "I had been keeping my NA membership a secret, but someone I had seen in meetings was friends with a rival at work. She told the rival and he told everyone. I was terrified. But the result was—nothing. Now I'm free to be myself; I don't have to hide anymore." It can be uncomfortable or even frightening to feel that we carry our anonymity as a secret. Not hiding means that we can be ourselves, and also that we are free to carry the message when we see an opportunity.

When we run into people we know from work or other contexts in NA meetings, we want to consider each other's anonymity. We might be comfortable sharing our membership with others, but that doesn't mean the other person is. Allowing each of us to experience our membership in our own way is part of the freedom we give one another. Just as we don't judge one another's desire to stop using, we cannot judge commitment or quality of membership based on a person's willingness to be known as a member.

Learning to choose wisely and appropriately is important. We may be the only example of recovery someone ever sees, and our behavior is a reflection of our message. We want to consider this when we wear or carry NA memorabilia or put an NA sticker on our car. We are letting people know something about ourselves, and we are telling them about the fellowship as well. Our message is carried not just by what we say, but also by what we do.

Likewise, each of us makes decisions for ourselves about what kind of environments we feel comfortable in. Some of us are never in the presence of drugs after we get clean; others of us find that our obligations to work or our families may expose us to people who are using. What one member sees as an unnecessary risk, another may find an essential part of integrating back into society. It is important to remember that we always have the option to leave if a situation has gotten uncomfortable.

When we share honestly about our lives, who we are and what we do become vital parts of our message of recovery. Our fellow members often take pride in our success, just as our family might. But we don't want to lose the foundation of equality that keeps us all alive and free. Knowing that each of us is no better or worse than any other member makes it easier to live with our past, and to begin to hope for our future. It also means that we can see our success as part of our lives, but not as our whole identity: A change in our status for better or worse doesn't have to destroy us. Our practice of anonymity means that we can continue to grow in good times and bad, and that we can continue to see the benefit of practicing a program of recovery even when our lives are extraordinary.

Honest self-assessment is essential to recovery, but it is only possible if we are vulnerable enough to let someone in. We choose those mirrors carefully, seeking those we can trust to be honest, helpful, and kind. This difficult process is made harder when we are admired for our accomplishments, profession, or social status; we may find that people are reluctant to tell us about our flaws. They may not even see them. When we treat a member as an icon rather than as another addict seeking recovery, we deprive them of the opportunity to experience the recovery they may desperately need. None of our members is more or less valuable than any other; when we forget this, we harm one another and the fellowship as a whole.

The Gift of Hope

We have so much to offer. We are good listeners, and we know how to find the strength and hope in our experience. We are on a path and are conscious of our journey. In our own way, we are each loving, caring, and generous. NA is boot camp for caring: We can learn more about empathy in our first year in NA than most people do in a lifetime. What we learn about living in NA is applicable outside as well, and we can be good friends to others whether they are in recovery or not. The tools and principles we learn here can serve others in and out of the fellowship. When we venture out, we get to discover how useful we can be.

We learn from each other's examples. Those who go before us clear the path we walk today; we walk in one another's footprints as we progress on our journey. We learn responsibility by watching others be responsible. Telling the truth about ourselves doesn't just set us free; our example frees others. Even in our most painful moments, we can still be a vision of what is possible. If we are willing to include the people we sponsor and draw them closer as we go through an ordeal, they can offer support and reassurance we dearly need. We also give them the chance to learn from our experiences—and our mistakes. We can be an example of strength and perseverance for others, and we can look to others for hope as well.

When we find our place, we fit like a piece in a puzzle. It feels right. "Recovering in complete creative freedom" means that we can listen to our heart and our Higher Power, and follow that path wherever it leads. The first time we believe we can stay clean, we begin to understand that we have choices about our lives. But living out our choices takes courage, patience, and perseverance. We have to be willing to hang in there when it gets hard, and keep going when we're not sure we're getting anywhere. We keep doing what's necessary to care for ourselves as we move forward. The same tools that brought us freedom in the beginning can keep working if we continue to use them with the same willingness.

We are loved and our lives have meaning today. We do remarkable things with our lives—sometimes by accomplishing big goals, and sometimes simply by being ourselves. A member complained to her sponsor that as a homemaker she felt she wasn't really doing enough with her life or her time, that maybe she should have done something more important. Her sponsor smiled. "Are you kidding? By breaking the cycle of addiction in your family, you're changing history!" Our greatest achievements may not be the things anyone else ever knows about: The simple fact that we survive our own stories is monumental. That we go on to help others and live lives we can be proud of is beyond our wildest dreams. Whatever we do, we make a difference in the world because we are clean.

7

The Journey Continues

Awakenings

A spiritual awakening is just that—an awakening. We still have to get out of bed. Some people awaken for just a moment and then doze off again. If we want to stay awake and alive, if we want the miracle of recovery to continue to unfold in our lives, we find ways to put this awakening into action. If we are not carrying the message, we go to sleep again.

We seem to awaken in stages, not all at once. We may not know it right away, but the first time we find hope is a spiritual awakening. Each of us experiences new awakenings as we examine our beliefs and practice living by them. Honesty, open-mindedness, and willingness are often the first spiritual principles we experiment with. We learn more principles as we go, and some become more important to us than others. Over time, we gain more experience with using them to guide our actions. Spirituality is progressive, dynamic, and creative. The foundation of our recovery is that we have to get out of ourselves in order to live.

In early recovery, many of us move back and forth between genuine excitement at our new possibilities and sorrow for what we have lost. Some of us describe early recovery as a "pink cloud," and others tell about a long season of grief. We experience many new feelings, sometimes very quickly. We grow and change, build and lose relationships, go to meetings, and we learn. Throughout our recovery we experience new awakenings, new surrenders, and new freedoms. The simple principles we learn when we are beginning our recovery take on deeper meaning as we practice them in our lives. Just when we think we know all that recovery has to offer, more is revealed—if we are willing to accept the gift.

There is no substitute for time in recovery. It gives us a chance to heal, grow up, start over, and build lives that matter to us and to the people around us. But time itself doesn't heal us, grow us up, or start us over. What matters most are the actions we take. Consistent application of the tools of recovery changes us. The process is ongoing. We don't just work the steps; we come to live them. They shape how we think, how we feel, and how we respond to the world. The steps teach us to grow up and help others. We learn to love ourselves by speaking the truth. Accepting our assets is part of our amends to ourselves, but more importantly, it begins the process by which we make our amends to society. Humility is honesty about who and what we are. We come to see how much we have and how much we have to offer. There is a difference between being in the program and living the program. When we come to an understanding of this program for ourselves, it becomes our own, and it becomes a part of us.

Building a spiritual life that we can grow with is a creative action. It requires that we practice, develop our beliefs, and apply them to our lives. Step Eleven does not say, "We maintain a conscious contact"; it says, "We sought … to improve our conscious contact…" When we practice our program, this relationship doesn't just get more important—it gets better. Our spiritual experience doesn't have to make sense to anyone but ourselves. Embracing the part of ourselves that is creative—that changes the things around us in a meaningful and positive way—is an act of self-acceptance that becomes visible in our lives. We discover that the things we care about and value the most reflect the will of our Higher Power for us.

Self-acceptance frees us to do the next right thing, or to wait peacefully for the next words or actions to emerge. When we are no longer in the middle of the storm, we begin to understand ourselves, our disease, and our recovery in different ways. We can be ourselves in the present moment without fear or apology, without the need for approval or justification.

When dancers move through space with intention and beauty, we say they are graceful. In the same way, when we move through our lives with intention and gratitude, we demonstrate grace; when we crash from one self-willed experience to another, creating damage and confusion, we are disgraceful. If we are willing to return to humility and gratitude, our lives get easier. Even when we can't identify the next right thing, we can generally see the next wrong thing and stay away from it. When our spirituality leads us, we can move through our lives with ease.

Our lives in recovery are so unlike what brought us here that we may not know what to do. Sometimes even achieving our goals can seem to make our lives unmanageable. Experience can be a mighty teacher. Awareness creates a foundation for new ideas; life provides opportunities to put that new information into action. Adapting to new information can take time. Awareness that we are in possession of a precious gift changes how we see ourselves and our world. We experience grace.

Joy and gratitude walk hand in hand. For some of us, joy is the sense that we are part of something much larger than ourselves, and more important than our immediate feelings and experiences. We matter, but we matter most when we are connecting with others. This deep sense of joy does not require that we be happy all the time. It's bigger than that. Humility means that we understand our place in the world; joy comes from seeing that we have a purpose. Being spiritually awake, we can see the miracles that surround us, even when life is difficult. Generosity of spirit is the antidote for loneliness and alienation.

Living Our Principles

Understanding is important, but it doesn't help much without application. We apply the principles, and we apply effort. We apply ourselves to changing our perspective and our lives. When things get difficult, it can be easy to forget that we already have a life we love and enjoy. We don't have to deny reality to have hope or gratitude. We feel what we feel, and we do the footwork anyway. We learn not to take our emotions quite so seriously. "My feelings aren't facts," said a member, "but I still feel them." When we choose not to look through the lens of resentment and entitlement, we can see the world as it is and find beauty in it even when it's challenging. Each day is filled with opportunities either to escape reality or to show up and live.

Each of us works our program differently, and it changes for each of us over time. It might mean that we are writing, serving, attending meetings—or just that we are practicing a conscious contact with our Higher Power. Whatever it means for us, we have a responsibility to walk our talk. The idea that "if you want what we have, do what we do" has no expiration date.

The awareness that we can always get better brings its own freedom. We can see the changes in our lives and in our thinking, and we know that recovery works for us. The more we know that, the more we can see what still needs to be done. We have ideas about what our lives are supposed to look like "by now," and we shame ourselves for not being there. We don't have to get caught up in ideas of where we "should be." This is an issue in early recovery, but it comes back as we get some cleantime. A member who was homeless on his twentieth anniversary was ashamed to celebrate. "What have I got to show the newcomer?" he asked. "That you can stay clean no matter what," came the reply. Acceptance frees us to share honestly about our lives without feeling that we have to fit into a model or be anyone other than who we are. Serenity doesn't mean that we don't experience dramatic events. It gives us the clarity of mind to go through them. No matter what happens, we can remain whole and joyful at our core.

Our understanding of the steps deepens, and we start to see the possibilities they offer in new ways. The more we trust, the more our eyes are opened. We are no longer so focused on what is wrong with us; we start to shift our attention to the assets we have and the hope we can see for ourselves. When we can separate hope from wishing or expectation, it stops feeling like such a setup. More and more we are driven by hope rather than fear. The gratitude we feel grows from relief at not having to use today to genuine appreciation for our lives as they are and as they can be. When we put gratitude into action, we see the world differently. A member shared: "My touch has come back, my smell and taste are alive. My children and grandchildren run into my arms and are safe there. People who come into my life go away with something good." The sense of wonder we experience in our own lives—as if we were seeing them for the first time—brings an array of feelings. Our hearts break for the harm we have caused, while at the same time we are filled with joy and gratitude for the gift of recovery.

It is such a relief to be able to feel good again. Even pain is okay sometimes—it helps us feel human. But sometimes it seems like we don't have our hand on the emotional volume knob. "When I started to feel, I had no control over my emotions," a member shared. "I learned different ways to deal with them over time. My sponsor taught me to name my feelings and had me create a written list of healthy things I could do when I was emotional." Our feelings won't consume us, even though it sometimes feels like they might. At some level it really doesn't matter what we feel. What matters is what we do. We no longer have to act on our impulses and emotions. We can make choices in our lives today about what we do and how we respond.

We may still get depressed or frightened or angry, but our feelings don't have to take possession of us anymore. When we realize we've survived every emotion we ever had, we start to believe that we are going to be alright even when we don't feel alright. Our best lessons often come by looking back at our own bad behavior. Our regret helps us to find compassion for others and a sense of possibility for our new way of life. Getting some perspective means that we can put a little distance between our thoughts, our feelings, and our actions. Our feelings won't kill us, but denying them might. It's usually when we're trying to avoid a feeling that we act out, creating damage and confusion to divert attention. Admitting our feelings, even when we're judging ourselves for having them, is one way we practice honesty.

We come to see our addiction in different ways and to recognize it in different feelings and behaviors. Sometimes it's as simple as obsession and compulsion, but we may also recognize it in a need to be in control, fear of being wrong, self-pity, and self-righteousness. We can see it in other behaviors as well, including conformity, mistrust, inability to feel love or sadness, and fear of change. A member shared: "I have worked the steps, and I have not worked the steps. And I have experienced the consequences of both." Our willingness to pay the price for acting out on our defects starts to fade. We learn to recognize our own disease as we get better at being aware of what's happening inside us. When we are better able to look at ourselves honestly and understand how we operate, it's easier for us to accept ourselves. Honest self-assessment requires a little detachment, so we can stop judging and become willing to change. Having compassion for others teaches us to have compassion for ourselves. Some of us ask ourselves how we would respond to a sponsee going through what we are struggling with.

We rely on a strong foundation, and we never stop working on it. We know what we can expect when we walk into an NA meeting, and that makes us feel safe and secure. We may resist changes to the format or style of our meetings even when they're a good idea, because we hold so tightly to that sameness. Making changes can be a challenge in other areas of our lives as well. When we're experiencing change, we want to hurry back to a place of comfort and familiarity. Allowing ourselves to have an emotional life without being controlled by our feelings is a new freedom.

Knowing our spirituality cannot be taken from us gives us permission to hope in a new way. Many of us are uncomfortable with hope. We have been so deeply disappointed in our lives that hope just feels like a bad idea. Some of us can't tell the difference between hope and wishing. But the hope we get in recovery is not that we will win the lottery or that our true love will return to us. Hope begins when we think that it might be possible for us to stop using against our own will and stay clean. We find it again and again as our journey continues: In the dark moments when we realize we can go on anyway, and in our triumphs—it is possible. It's possible we can break the cycle, it's possible we can exceed our dreams, it's possible that we are much more than we ever gave ourselves credit for. Each time we realize it's possible, our faith grows stronger. Hope doesn't end. No matter how much better or worse it gets, we know that there is still reason to look forward. We begin to experience unconditional hope.

The Lifelong Practice of Surrender

Our understanding of surrender may change over time, but our need for it does not. In the beginning, surrender might just be about not using drugs. As time goes by, we start to see other ways our addiction plays out in our lives. We become willing to surrender other behaviors, sometimes one by one. We come to understand that using—whatever we are using—is just a symptom of our problem, which is spiritual in nature. Gradually we start to let go of the things that drive us to act out: denial, anger, resentment, the need to be right, the feelings of superiority or inferiority, shame, remorse, and fear.

As our understanding of the First Step grows, we surrender more deeply. Our trust grows, and we become a little more willing to let go. We can see more areas of our lives where we still cling to the illusion of control. Surrender rarely looks appealing in the beginning, but it takes us progressively less time to notice when what we are doing isn't working. At first we may let go only when we are beaten, but our tolerance for pain diminishes as we recover. We are less willing to go along with things that wound our spirit. As we have more experience with the hope and healing that follows, we can recognize surrender as a way we put our feet back on the ground. The shift from thinking that we surrender to our disease to realizing that we can surrender to our recovery is a spiritual awakening in itself.

Changing our perception is like seeing the world through a different pair of glasses. Surrender is a shift in perception: We are no longer looking for an angle at which we can take control. Honesty can shift our perception: It opens us to the truth. We concern ourselves less with what other people might think of us, and find instead that we are answerable to our own morals and values. We begin to see more clearly what it might mean to live according to the will of our Higher Power. Each time we surrender, our world opens up a little more. We can see past our obsession and accept the possibility of a change in our perception. We might take a deep breath and ask ourselves what would happen if we just let go. Our faith grows through our experience, and gives us the opportunity to see our lives from a different perspective. As we gain experience, we don't feel as much like we have to go out on a limb to act on our beliefs. We begin to trust that the result of letting go will not be a calamity. A series of spiritual awakenings add up to a steady faith.

Fear is a natural feeling. The question is what we do with it. Steps Three and Eleven allow us to invite a loving Higher Power into our decisions, and Step Ten helps us to check ourselves as we go. We are often the last ones to see or acknowledge our own growth. When we see other members recovering and their lives improving, we are reminded that the same is happening for us. As our awareness deepens, we continue to find areas of our lives that need work. As we change, we adjust. And as we adjust, our balance shifts and we change some more. Feeling like we know it all is often followed by the feeling that we know nothing. It's a nice feeling, for the moment that it lasts—and then we get to learn more about surrender.

We learn not to take ourselves too seriously. At the end of the road, nothing was funny anymore, but as we let go of worry, shame, anger, and confusion, we start to relax. One of the gifts of recovery is regaining our sense of humor. It comes and goes, of course, but when we lose our sense of humor it's a pretty good sign that we could benefit from a change in perspective. A member shared about a woman in her home group whose laugh would fill the room: "Her laughter gave me hope. It had so much love and self-acceptance in it. You could hear the joy." We can laugh because things are meaningful, or because we know that it's going to be okay. We can see the magic and the irony in our lives, and enjoy it. Lightening up is a necessary step on the way to enlightenment! The humor we find in one another's stories is one way we know we are in the right place. What's funny to us tends to change as we grow. We are less amused by the suffering of others, and more able to see the lighter side of heavy situations.

Complacency

Complacency is a watchword for all of us, but it shows up in different ways at different times. Most of all, what we know about complacency is that we rarely recognize it when we're in it. In some ways, there's not much sense in trying to talk about it before we experience it. We always believe our own experience will be different. Most of us don't recognize it until it hurts.

We may not know we have a reservation until we bump up against it. Reservations can be surprising—not what we predicted at all. Some of us struggle with pride and complacency when we finish the steps. Others lose hope when we are going through a hard time. Some of us have shared that it got hard when things got good: Our lives get better, and we think, "Okay, I'm done." Complacency lies in the gulf between desperation and passion. Not only do we risk losing what we have; we miss out on the opportunity to get even better. Not seeing the hope that lies before us, we stop seeing the fear that lingers behind us. Rather than moving from desperation to passion, we move from desperation to complacency. It may be better than what we had, but we are still shortchanging ourselves.

Our stories of complacency are much the same. We get lost in work or worship or some other activity, think that NA is stifling or limiting our growth in some way, or that we have "grown past" this recovery stuff. We lose a sponsor or move, and just never reconnect. Sometimes it's a gradual process: We drift away from friends, stop going to meetings, get busy at work, or start developing resentments. A little at a time, we stop working on our recovery and our disease starts gaining a foothold. We can lose everything to a failure of imagination. Thinking that we no longer have to be vigilant about meeting attendance, step work, or sponsorship can lead us to predictable places. "I was on the road a lot for work," one member shared, "and it stopped being a big deal to not show up." We can't see how addiction is affecting us, especially when the destruction looks different than before. It is possible to lull ourselves to sleep in this program and think we are still awake. The living skills we gain in recovery can become part of our denial structure. It's not that everyone who does this relapses, but it seems that nearly everyone who relapses after staying clean for a while shares this part of the story.

The risk of relapse doesn't end when we get some cleantime. A member with many years clean admitted: "To this day, I still try to talk myself out of qualifying for this program. The majority of my problems are related to my self-centeredness and immaturity, and I want to separate that from my addiction. I start thinking, 'You're older now, wiser and more mature. Real addicts don't stay clean this long.' My own cleantime becomes a reservation." Some of us fear contentment or serenity because it might look like, or lead to, complacency. If there's nothing left to fight against, will there be anything left to strive for? Finding the balance is a challenge. We can slow down without stopping. We learn to be content without being complacent—we can be very happy with our lives as they are, and still not stop doing the basics.

Just as a battery can't recharge itself, chances are we can't put the spark back into our own recovery without some outside power. Participation in the life of our fellowship keeps NA alive—but it also keeps the spirit of recovery alive within us. "I didn't know how much faith I had until I lost it," a member shared. "Recovery started to seem meaningless. Dry and cynical, I couldn't check the negativity by myself. I had to seek out opportunities to witness the miracle happening." Connecting with those who have enthusiasm and hope is a beginning. Thinking about recovery never helps as much as getting out and taking action, especially when we don't want to. When what we're doing isn't working, we stop. But when what we're doing is halfway working, we tend to keep going even if it's uncomfortable, because we're used to it. Sometimes it seems like the longer we are clean, the less we are willing. Just like in the beginning, we may have to fight our impulses and make ourselves do what we know is right.

Celebrations can propel us out of complacency, and many members find that a good convention or retreat can get the gratitude flowing again. Celebrating the anniversary of an addict who is important to us reminds us what a miracle it is that we are still here. A service commitment gets us to a meeting when desire doesn't. Sharing with a newcomer can bring us out of our funk; carrying the message reminds us that we have a message. Sometimes we just have to get honest about where we are, and let go of the belief that we're not supposed to share about feeling bad or wanting to use if we have the most cleantime in the room. Even when we don't want to, we know what to do: If you're feeling complacent, come place your end in a seat. The message is waiting.

Setting Ourselves Apart

Whether they had three years or thirty, we recall the members who had the most time when we got clean. We may or may not have liked them, but still they were important to us. We depend on those with more cleantime to teach us and energize our recovery, but eventually we find that we are standing where they once did. We look around for the oldtimers and notice—we're them. We are grateful for those who are still with us, but we must also be open to learning from those who come after us, or we will get very lonely. Anonymity means that we are all equals in NA, no matter how much cleantime we have. Remembering that can be hard sometimes and we may need to remind one another that it's true. We can get caught up in expectations of where we should be or what we should know with our cleantime.

Honesty, humility, and a healthy sense of humor can help us navigate through these challenges. We learn to help members answer their own questions, and not to feed the image of ourselves as an authority figure. The fact that people ask for our advice doesn't mean we are qualified to give it. We share our experience, strength, and hope, but we are careful with our opinions—especially when we know they're taken seriously. It's nice to feel important or respected, but we indulge in it at our peril. When we allow our fellow members to believe that we no longer have needs, the result is that we have nowhere to go when we are in pain.

No amount of cleantime can make us immune to our disease or exempt us from the challenges of life. Recovery is an every day, just for today process. A relationship with our Higher Power requires ongoing conscious contact, and ongoing growth requires that we remain teachable. "Keeping it green" means that we are still in process, still willing to change and grow and work on ourselves. We keep our recovery alive by feeding it. If we are not getting ongoing support and nourishment, we get depleted. It is our responsibility to find that support, even if it means we need to reach out across long distances.

The simple fact is, if we stay clean, one day we will be the one with the most time in the room. It's a gift, a responsibility, and a pitfall, all at once. Many members share that it's easy to feel separate when there is a gap in cleantime. Sometimes being the member in the room with the most time feels as daunting as walking into our first ninety meetings. We may feel like the newer people don't understand us, or that there is no one we can reach out to for help. When we are more aware of our responsibility than of our ability to get what we need, we feel isolated. A member shared that being viewed as an elder was uncomfortable: "I'm the one people come to with questions, and I don't feel equal. It's not about feeling 'better than,' but separate from." We don't always know when or how we will find ourselves in trouble, and we certainly don't know who is going to get us out. We find people who have what we want, regardless of cleantime. It's one of the most beautiful things about NA—someone always steps up to the plate. It's often not whom we expect. We do not have the luxury of choosing who is allowed to save our lives.

It is sometimes said that our emotional development stops when we start using, and that when we get clean, we pick up where we left off. It may or may not be that simple, but the fact is, most of us have some serious maturing to do in recovery, and we spend many years in the process. Most of us go through some time in our recovery when we are desperate for recognition and approval. Really basic questions become important. Am I visible? Am I heard? Do I matter? It is neither selfless nor anonymous. It may even be destructive, but it's frequently a part of our process.

It can be appealing to get up on a pedestal. Actually, many people on pedestals don't volunteer for it—and once we are up there, we may not know how to get down. When people treat us differently because of our cleantime or our service, it can get very lonely and very strange. The less we believe we deserve that attention, the more insecure we get—and the more approval we seek. When we are past that point in our lives, we can look back and see the humor in wanting to be a celebrity in an anonymous fellowship. But when we're in that place, it can feel like the most important thing in the world. A member with a lot of time said: "When I was new, you loved me but you didn't baby me. Don't do it now. It's condescending and it separates me from any other recovering addict." It's the separation that makes that position so dangerous.

As willing as some of us are to put people up on pedestals, others of us are even more eager to knock them down. We can be mean and spiteful, judgmental and harsh. Kicking the pedestal doesn't help anybody to change. A member shared, "Any time I've been crazy, when it all came crashing down, the people I came to weren't the mean, judgmental ones, but the ones who had been honest and loving." If we want to help someone down, waiting may be the best thing we can do. Time is more powerful than we are. We may or may not be the people to carry the message to a friend who forgets we're all equal here. It may or may not be our job to confront someone. Pulling someone's covers is an incredibly intimate experience. If we don't pay attention to circumstances, what we do may simply be violent. Being humble and honest is a better approach than trying to be someone else's conscience.

The fact is that we do not have to live perfectly to carry a message. More importantly, we don't get to choose who deserves to be a vehicle for something greater. We can carry a message even if we're not quite living it, and some people might be helped by what we share. But inside, it is slowly destructive. When our expectations start to make our choices for us, we can become disillusioned, disconnected, and fearful of the very thing that saves our lives.

Newer members expect oldtimers to be stable, grounded, and principled—and often we are. But there will always be times when we fall short. Once we lose the feeling that we are an ordinary "garden variety addict" like everyone else, it can be hard to regain it. We seek out others who have had that experience, and ask them how they handled it. We are addicts in recovery, doing our best to learn how to live. When we remember that, the rest falls into place.

Consciousness can change through its surroundings, with no action needed. "At some point," shared a member, "I had all the attention I could stand, and I started pushing the next guy up front." This is our learning ground, and sometimes we make a mess in the process. It can be a wonderful aid in helping us get free of our need for approval. "I really, finally, don't care what people think of me," said an older member. Ultimately we see that when we are secure in ourselves, we carry a message without saying a word.

Time is time, and in the end what it gets us is a seat in a meeting like everyone else. We come to enjoy our own anonymity, even if people still sometimes call us out as special. When we share from the heart, we generally don't remember much about what we share. We disconnect from ego and something else happens: The truth comes through us, and it takes on a life of its own. We hear the gratitude after we speak and know it's not about us. It's the love that came through us that teaches us all something in the moment. The love that we feel in the room is more powerful than any words that are shared. When we glimpse what it is we are allowed to be a channel for, we are truly humbled.

The best way to model recovery is to walk the walk, and show up honest and real. When we are sort of showing up and we're sort of honest, we're "sort of" in danger. We need to remember that our first job, always, is to allow our own lives to be saved. Sharing what is real for us is a benefit to our recovery and a responsibility to those who follow, even if it doesn't make us look good. A member shared: "I remember the people who were here when I got here and how they bared their souls in meetings, and I follow suit. It's a benefit to my recovery and a responsibility to those who follow." We learn from each other's experience. Sharing our journey with others is how we teach and learn at the same time. Honest sharing is always attractive, even when we are sharing some really unattractive stuff. When we are honest and open, it resonates with people. When we are humble, they feel it—and so do we.

Keeping It Real

We all need to reenergize ourselves sometimes—physically, emotionally, and spiritually. We separate these parts of ourselves so we can talk about them more easily, but really they are all connected. Just as we may be much more emotionally sensitive when we are physically tired, we find that when we are emotionally exhausted we're prone to get physically sick. When we are spiritually exhausted we can feel deeply insecure. Some of us are at our best when we are moving and busy; others of us recharge when we're alone and quiet. It may be as simple as sitting down for a brief meditation, or showing up at a meeting.

Reaching out might be the best thing we can do for ourselves—and for those around us. Seeing the program work in another person's life affirms our commitment and gives us hope. "At ten years clean I hit a wall," said a member. "For me the turnaround was a group of newcomers whose passion and intensity woke me up. It was the same passion that kept me clean in the beginning." We can recognize the change in others before we see it in ourselves.

Some of us thrive on working with newcomers. We only keep what we have by giving it away, but we don't know what we have until we start to give. In the moment, dealing with someone who is struggling or in pain, we find resources within us that we never knew about. When we see someone really get it and take off, it gives us a gratitude we never thought possible. We don't get to choose who gets recovery. It's not up to us to choose who to help. It can be hard sometimes to watch the spark land, flash, and go out—over and over again. When we show up and do our part, the message gets carried. "When I'm helping someone through the steps, I feel like an instrument of my Higher Power's will," a member said. "I'm not in charge. My responsibility is just to stay close."

The work we have done to build our fellowship means that a lot more experience, strength, and hope is available to newer people than "back in the day." But the skills we develop helping an NA community get started may be different from those we need to maintain unity and stability once that community is established. We are liable to feel left out or left behind. The trouble with being called a "dinosaur" is that we know they are extinct. Staying involved helps us to grow and requires us to change.

It may sound odd, but we are also responsible to let ourselves be outgrown. It can be a challenge when we've been sponsoring someone for a while to accept when they decide to move on. We take comfort in the thought that, if they are taking responsibility for their recovery, we did our

job. As a fellowship, too, we can see our growth. Those of us who have been here since the very early days can see it in a particular way that is bitter and sweet. The fact that NA changes and the patterns and habits at the meeting are different can be an excuse to leave. It's another reservation we couldn't predict. When we stay involved with a living, growing, and changing fellowship, we don't notice so much. But if we move or take a break, the changes can be startling.

NA changes. People come and go. But we change, too. The time we have available, our relationships with others, the way we're comfortable serving or participating—they all change naturally over the course of our lives. When the steps are an ongoing part of our lives, we are called on pretty regularly to examine our lives and see what is working and what can be improved. It's natural that we will take a hard look sometimes at NA, too. We consider our fellowship, how we see ourselves in it, and our beliefs about it. It can be very uncomfortable and frightening. When we give ourselves the space to examine our commitment, we can be honest about it—just like in any other relationship.

When our beliefs and perceptions are changing, we can experience pain and confusion that leave us feeling isolated. We can be cut off from others, but also from ourselves and our Higher Power. Sharing with others at these moments is critical. It can be surprising how welcome that sharing is. When we are honest and real, we connect with people. When we have a lot of cleantime, we can get caught up in what we think we are supposed to share in meetings. When the message we carry is an honest reflection of our experience rather than what we imagine other people want to hear, the truth can set all of us free.

There are many ways to think about our disease. Some say that addiction is a severe case of the human condition. We struggle with the same fears and insecurities that everyone else does, but we experience them to a degree that makes us willing to die to escape them. Other members say that addiction is a shame-based disease. At the core of our diseased thinking is the belief that something is wrong with us. When we are looking at the world, or at ourselves, through eyes of shame, everything we see is further evidence that we are wrong or bad, or that we cannot be restored to sanity. We describe our struggle differently as our relationship to it changes.

Some people say that addiction is a disease of nostalgia: We glamorize the past and terrorize the present. We may not recognize it in ourselves, but when we hear people we think of as newcomers complaining that "it's not like it used to be" about what seems to us to have been the recent past, we can start to find the humor in it.

Something special happens when we first get clean. Our desperation and the total commitment we make in the beginning combine to create a very precious and important time in our lives. It's never the same as our first home group, our first real connection to a sponsor, or that initial group of friends we ran with in early recovery. But the fact that it's not the same doesn't mean it's not as good. A member shared: "When I let myself approach my recovery like a newcomer, I don't struggle so much with the differences between how it is and how I think I remember it was. I can be present today without getting lost in nostalgia or comparison." Allowing our recovery to change as we change can be difficult, but it's what makes staying in NA possible—and productive.

The things we do when our NA community is small are the basics. Just like in our personal recovery, if we get away from the basics, we may have a hard time getting back to them. Meetings get complacent, too. When we get lazy, the message gets watered down. When we see that happening in our groups, we have a responsibility—not to complain or chastise, but to get busy. Sometimes starting step studies or literature discussions can help bring the focus of meetings back to recovery. Some of the most important work we do is at our home group. Participation at our home group makes it feel like it's really home. "I wish I could say my actions are selfless," one member confessed, "but deep down I know that my goal is to keep my home group alive so that I can keep coming back." We feel good about meetings where we feel loved and accepted, and where we can be useful. Little things like calling members when they don't show up can really reinvigorate a home group. Not giving up on each other matters—whether or not we are just getting clean. We teach by example. When we share honestly and openly from the heart about recovery, we carry a more powerful message than we ever do when we're preaching or lecturing.

NA is different from place to place, and at different stages of growth. There is no model of the recovering fellowship. In some places, families are very involved. In some places, we take members into our homes to detox. In some places, tough love is the norm, and we tell people to sit down and shut up; in other places, we encourage one another to talk it out. The principles are consistent, but how we practice them can vary widely. The key is that we practice them, that our unity comes first, and that we keep our focus on our primary purpose: to carry the message to the addict who still suffers. Politics and popularity distract us from our purpose. When NA members forget that our personal recovery depends on NA unity, both are in jeopardy. NA communities do sometimes wither and die. It's a tragedy we can learn from. We have a tendency to believe that things which are free have no value, when in fact they may be precious beyond any measure. When we recognize that our fellowship is in trouble, we must take loving action. Our lives depend on it.

Being of Service

The desire to be of service changes our relationship to the world. It's not just in NA that we are loving and giving. We connect to the love that surrounds us by practicing loving actions, and being open to receiving the same. Being willing to accept help is a form of giving. It can be uncomfortable to admit a need, or to ask for help. When we allow another person to step up and help us, we give them a chance to express their own love and generosity. When we reach out to help, we receive much more than we give. In some places, after the closing prayer at the meetings, NA members say, "Keep coming back!" In other places, they say, "Go help someone!" Both come from the understanding that when we give, and when we allow others to give, we find a connection to a power greater than ourselves.

Service is not a position in a committee; it is a posture in the heart. It's a way of life we can practice in all our affairs. It can be as simple as holding a door open, or as complicated as helping a loved one in the last stages of life. Our relationship to service and the way we express it changes as our humility deepens. The desire to serve is a manifestation of freedom from self. Anonymity is a key principle in selfless service. When we learn to give selflessly, in service to those who suffer and to a power greater than ourselves, we find happiness, purpose, and dignity.

Whether we give back best in structured service, one-on-one, or somewhere in between, being of service is a matter of principle for us. Practicing and teaching principle-based service is both a way we carry the message and a way we receive the gifts that recovery has to offer us. Service connects us to the fellowship and helps keep us connected and involved even when we're not at the top of our game. Having a commitment to open the door at a meeting once a week can be the difference between staying involved and slipping away. Early on, service is a way we start to feel useful and wanted. Later on, being of service gives us a reason to keep coming back even when we don't feel like it.

The therapeutic value of one addict helping another is a two-way street. It doesn't matter who is doing the giving or the taking. We are all equally entitled to ask and to provide, and wherever we are in the exchange, we benefit. We no longer have to weigh and balance who is getting more or less, whether we are doing enough or being taken for a ride. The truth is, we're all looking for motivation, inspiration, a spark that will catch fire in us. A good meeting, a powerful Twelfth Step call, a convention or campout can leave us feeling filled up, knowing that just for a moment we were right where we needed to be. That feeling is addictive. Once we know we can feel that good, we want more. We are willing to slog through the hard times because we know, if we keep doing it, we're going to feel that complete again. It's not an illusion, like it was when we were using. It's the very real understanding that, just for today, what we do matters to someone.

Service changes our relationship to our own lives. We learn to put love and gratitude into action, and when we mobilize our good feelings they have a way of spreading through all our affairs. We are confronted with our defects—and with each other's—and we find a way to work through them. "The first time I chaired a committee, I discovered the true meaning of principles before personalities. Boy, did I grow!" a member chuckled. In service we meet others who are passionate about their recovery, and that excitement keeps us energized. For those of us who have always had difficulty fitting in, service can give us something to do—and a reason to stay to the end of the meeting, the workshop, or the dance. In the meantime, we make the connections that change our lives. We learn about recovery in the process of serving, but also in the margins of the service we do: In the talks while we're setting up or cleaning up for an event, or on the long ride to a service commitment, we make connections with others who are serious about recovery. A member shared: "I've had to close my mouth when I wanted to open it and open my mouth when I wanted to close it. I've had to try doing new things and stop doing old things that are no longer working. I've had to learn to ask for help, to delegate responsibilities, take risks, and share. I've had to clean up some disgusting messes—both literal and figurative. Why do I serve? It reinforces all the work I do in the steps."

Some of us jump into service with both feet. We involve ourselves in just about every facet of what is going on, only to be rebuffed by members who have different ideas

about how things need to be done. Or we make so many commitments that we cannot possibly keep them all, and gradually get overwhelmed and resentful. We get discouraged and withdraw. We go from caring too much to not caring at all and back again. We find ourselves outside the fellowship we love, looking in. We get lost in self-pity—after all, didn't we give it our best effort? Times like these try the spirits of even our most seasoned members. We may need to step aside from that type of service for a moment and focus on our primary purpose.

When we let go of that distraction, our recovery can begin a new chapter. In the meantime, we stay clean, and a lot of good can get done. The solution begins in the Tenth Step. We reflect on our motives in service. Are we trying to force our view of how NA does things on others, or do we truly want to be helpful? Can we step out of ourselves long enough to allow someone else to have a chance sometimes? Our experience gives us knowledge of what has and has not worked. We can share that without trying to control the outcome. When we start taking it all very personally, we might want to consider whether it's time to step back. Knowing when to let go—of a point, a decision, or a position—takes prayer and practice. Rotation is an important principle in service for our own well-being, and for our fellowship as well.

Service can be an escape, or it can give us access to new parts of ourselves by allowing skills and interests to surface. When we think we're climbing a ladder, using our position as proof of some kind of success, that's just ego in action. But when we are giving back out of gratitude, selflessly and with the best interests of the whole at heart, we find that the experience can be as rewarding as it is productive. When we are spiritually awake, we need to be of service—and we have to do the step work to handle it.

We find a balance between service inside and outside NA as well. We care for one another in little ways—taking someone to a meeting, or bringing a meal to a sick friend. The program allows each of us to find the ways we are most comfortable giving, and the ways we are most comfortable asking for help. We confront our limitations, including the limits of our compassion, and learn to be realistic about what we can and cannot do.

When we have experience in service, we can be a resource and a mentor for others. We do that in a spirit of humility when we are committed to bringing more members into the process without retaining control. Patience, kindness, and trust are key to the process. If we treat others with trust and respect, we are likely to receive it in turn. We can lead by example, helping to guide discussion and focus energy without trying to influence the outcome. Participating without seeking the illusion of control sets the model for the rest of our lives. In whatever capacity we find ourselves, we serve NA with dedication and love when we serve with humility. Although we sometimes associate leadership with a lack of humility, for us it's refusing to serve at all that fosters our egoism and impatience. Service is always humbling. We learn to be servants. We walk through all of our ego stuff on the way. When we forget that we are just a small part of a greater whole, we are in trouble.

There are some words we use differently in NA than in the rest of the world. When we talk about addiction, for example, we are addressing a spiritual disease that

affects all areas of our lives. When we share about sanity, we're not interested in clinical definitions: We look to our own experience for a practical understanding that works for us. And when we talk about leadership in NA, we're not implying that some members have more power or authority than others. Leadership here is about sharing our experience in a spirit of humility and unity. We practice leadership in NA by serving selflessly. Whatever our service, we remember the suffering addict in all that we do, and we practice acceptance, courage, and action.

Responsibility is one of the most important principles we practice in NA, and service is one of the best ways we learn to practice it. Service keeps us involved with and surrounded by recovery, and it gives us opportunities to practice acceptance as well. By sharing our experience with other addicts, we gain a deeper understanding of ourselves. Seldom do addicts stay clean for long without practicing selfless service in one form or another. NA gives freely, but there's only so much we can simply take from the program. After a while, the rewards are not from what we are given but from what we give. The real work begins here, and not all of us are up to it. Reaping rewards means we must sow the seeds through action. There is responsibility in recovery, and it begins with taking responsibility for our recovery.

Sometimes just being accountable to something is rewarding. For those of us who don't have a lot of experience being responsible, this can be a really good lesson. Others have far too much experience being responsible, and service work teaches us to let go. Flexibility, tolerance, and balance are principles we learn to practice as we serve.

We learn to practice unity, even when it's uncomfortable, and we get to exercise our courage. "All my life I felt less than," a member shared. "A stranger would frown at me and I would have a bad day. Service helped me feel worthy."

Principles, Practice, and Perspective

NA service must always be done in the spirit of carrying the message to the addict who still suffers. This is our fellowship's primary purpose, and when we deviate from that we open the door to distracting influences. But there is rarely a time when our motives are entirely pure. Selfless service is our goal, but one of the things that makes service so rewarding is the knowledge that we are valuable and useful. It's not that the service we do is either entirely selfless or all about getting an ego-fix. The work we do can keep us together while we're waiting to feel good about ourselves. Our acceptance of that allows us to improve rather than to pretend we have it all together. It's not selfish to know that having a purpose makes us feel better. If we are acting in goodwill—doing the right thing for the right reasons—we are sure to benefit. Each of us has something to give, and allowing us to do that is part of helping each other to recover. It's an ongoing process. We find a niche for ourselves, learn to be comfortable there, outgrow it, and find a new one. Each time we learn something about ourselves, and often we learn to do something new. A member shared, "It seems like the more experience I get, the more inexperienced I realize I am."

Another member looked back on her introduction to service: "There was arguing, politics, agendas, and overall chaos. Yet from the moment the meeting started, I felt the love. Being new, it was exactly what I was used to, and I felt like I fit in."

That is not to say that disorder for its own sake is a good idea. But just like in our personal recovery, the hard parts are often where the lessons are. Letting new people serve allows more people to learn from the experience of serving. It also opens us to new ideas and new ways of doing things. There can be value in reinventing the wheel, even if it can seem like a pretty inefficient way to do business. We each learn from going through the process, and sometimes we also get a better wheel.

Everything changes—that's good news and bad news. Growing through the changes doesn't necessarily mean agreeing with them. But good-natured flexibility is a key to happy recovery. We try to have faith in the long view. It might be evolution or growing pains, but it's not necessarily ours to figure out. We don't have a crystal ball. An uncomfortable outcome is a phase in our development, not the end of our story. It's true in our personal recovery, and it's true in our fellowship as well. We grow and change, and our needs grow and change too. If we are involved in starting NA in a particular area, it can be very uncomfortable when that area settles into being a community. If we are involved in a particular kind of service for a long time, it can be difficult to allow others to step in and to accept that there is more than one way to do the job. When our identity gets wrapped up in how it used to be, we can't reach out in the same way. It's harder to ask for help because "they do it wrong," and it's hard to carry a message because our disappointment is so evident.

The fact that NA is different than it used to be is a consequence of our success and our growth. And chances are it's not really *that* different. The basics don't change.

The message we carry doesn't change. The things we need to do to stop using, lose the desire, and find a new way to live really don't change. Because we feel safe in the rooms, we feel like we know our place and we don't want anything to change. But when what we know best isn't wanted or needed in the same way, it's hard not to take it personally. We can have a fit when the chairs are rearranged at our home group. Learning to work with new people, trying new ways of doing things, can be painful and awkward. We allow one another to feel like we have a place in service and in the fellowship when we make it open and welcoming. Just saying "please" and "thank you" can make all the difference in the world.

If we embrace the principles of recovery, we naturally embrace the fellowship and help it to grow. Each of us does this in our own way. We may love and nourish our home group. We may start a meeting. Some of us are exceptional at working with new members. Others of us are great at communication. We may enjoy putting on events, or making beautiful websites. When service is in our heart, we find ways to be useful just as we are. The service that we do may never involve being "voted in" to anything. When we value one another's experience and work to make service fun, interesting, and inclusive, we find that there really is a place at the table for all of us. Just as service helps each of us grow, we need everyone's involvement to ensure that we are carrying our message as well and as widely as we can.

When we trust the Second Tradition, we can allow ourselves and others to make mistakes. Sometimes the mistakes we make in service—as in our lives—bring us to the next place we need to go. Trusting the Second Tradition gives us hope. We know that a loving God is in charge, and that the process is alive no matter what happens. Our judgments can interfere with the message getting through. We don't have to be the best person in the room to be the best person for the job. Part of making service attractive is finding a place for the people who are attracted to it.

It's essential in whatever way we give back that we are able to share with others and to cooperate, and these are not skills most of us bring to the rooms with us. Service teaches us to communicate, and it can be one of the most frustrating lessons we ever go through. Over and over we find ourselves in the position that we think we are offering information, and others seem not to get it—or not remember having gotten it.

Communication is always about more than the information being relayed. How we communicate cannot be separated from what we communicate. Taking a look at the difference between what we are saying, what is heard, and how people are responding to us can be the beginning of real change in all our relationships. In service and in our lives, we offer information to people in different ways. When we throw it at them, they always get upset. Too often, we offer information and expect people to know why they should be interested in it. There is life beyond the information; there's a reason the information we're presenting matters, and it's up to us to bring that forward. When we offer information without inspiration, people stop listening. The result is that we cut each other out of a conversation that really needs all of us.

The Second Tradition teaches us that a loving God may be expressed through our group conscience. Each of us is responsible to ensure that all of us have the information we need and the ability to share freely, so that the genius that develops through us has a chance to be heard. When we regard one another with respect, we open the door to a different kind of communication. When we practice attraction in our service, we work to make sure that it is as open, inclusive, and welcoming as it can possibly be. When our common welfare comes first, it shows.

We may each have our own ideas about issues and how to manage them, but our principles remind us that our ideas are not the only ones that matter. Bringing alternatives to the table, even if we don't agree with them, can help broaden a group's options. Often the best possible solution emerges in the process of coming to consensus, so it's up to us to give the group as much information as we can. Yielding to group conscience when we feel strongly provides an opportunity to experience trust. When we can believe that everyone in a disagreement is acting from a position of goodwill, we can be a little more willing to let go. When we can see past our own desires and accept where the group is, the quality of our relationship to our fellowship, group, or service committee is not conditional on getting our own way.

Finding a loving way to address differences of opinion or experience in NA gives us tools to reach out differently in the rest of our lives. We learn in the process that communication is at the heart of forgiveness. We can hang on for years to a resentment that could have been resolved with a simple conversation. Facing uncomfortable situations and taking loving action is a demonstration of maturity and grace. Emotional maturity is our reward for letting go of anger and resentment.

We don't get to choose our next generation in Narcotics Anonymous. It can be surprising who stays clean and who doesn't. We have had the experience of burying someone who looked like the "most likely to succeed," and of celebrating the anniversary of the craziest long shot in the room. As we stay around NA, we have a tendency to think that the members who are newer than us don't have the kind of foundation or experience we do. It's our responsibility to share what we were given, and to ensure that NA continues to grow. An experienced member suggested, "They are going to bring their experience to this program that saves my life, so I better be sure they have what they need to save me."

The fact that the fellowship is alive is evidence that this program works, and that it's still working. Our task is to trust that evidence more than our fear or our rigid beliefs of how it should be done. If we are doing it right, we will grow beyond what we know now—individually and as a group. When we have faith that our services really are guided by a loving Higher Power, we can let go and allow the process to unfold. Success comes when we work together toward a solution. There are times when mistakes are simply going to be made: We speak our piece and get out of the way. We find ways to stay involved that allow us to be useful and appreciate service. It may be constructive for us sometimes to take a break from the kind of service that involves committees and decisions, and come back to the front lines and the phonelines. Reaching a hand to the addict in need is the most important thing we do. When we shift our focus to the front door, our squabbles and resentments fade away. When we carry the message, we get the message. The message is freedom, and the ties that bind are pure love.

Love

The spirit of love that we express in NA is the most powerful thing we have. The Basic Text describes it as "the flow of life energy from one person to another," and we see this in action when we watch an addict come back to life in the rooms. The hugs we give are an instrumental part of our method and our experience. NA is all about love.

When we are practicing Step Twelve to the best of our ability, love becomes central to all that we do—there is no more powerful antidote to the despair and self-destruction of addiction. The compassion that we feel for the newcomer is something we learn to extend to our families, to those around us, and eventually, to ourselves. Some say that ultimately Step Twelve becomes about reaching out to anyone who is suffering. Certainly we cannot look away as we once did. Still, we can sometimes have an easier time offering compassion to newcomers than to oldtimers who are struggling.

Unity is a practice of love. We rise above our judgments and come together no matter what. In the process, we learn forgiveness and reconciliation. We don't always forgive before we start to work together again, but we are obliged to make peace because we cannot easily avoid one another. Forgiveness is an action and a decision. We need a lot of forgiveness, and we also get to provide it. Forgiving is its own reward. We start to find peace within ourselves. When we are free of guilt, shame, and resentment, our minds can be still.

Some of us struggle to give ourselves permission to be happy. We may not think we deserve it, or we may fear that we will stop working on ourselves. Some of us have been unhappy for so long that it feels uncomfortable to let go of our bitterness. When we treat happiness as a spiritual principle, we can see its relationship to humility. Our ability to enjoy our lives is directly related to our willingness to let go of our self-obsession. If we think of happiness as a spiritual asset, we can see it as both a gift and a goal. We work toward it by letting go of those things that we can see standing in its way, and leave the rest to a power greater than ourselves. Humility and empathy are essential to a rewarding spiritual life. As we find the deep joy that comes to us through our practice of compassion, we find that happiness is much more available to us. "I had to make a decision to be happy," said one member, "but making that decision in a way that could really work meant having a foundation on which that happiness could rest."

Walking through our own challenges helps us to find compassion for ourselves and others. As we develop our ability to feel and express empathy, we come to realize that the same spirit dwells in all of us, and that none of us is more or less important than another. We are all sick and suffering sometimes, no matter how long we have been clean. We all bring hope and answers sometimes, even when we don't feel it ourselves. One day clean is a miracle, whether or not it's ever followed by another. When we see a member experience a real breakthrough with 20, or 30, or more years clean, we can see that, truly, recovery never stops.

Love is an action word. Loving action takes many forms. Sometimes it's a warm hug; sometimes it's telling someone the cold, hard truth. But when we act from love, with the intention of loving, it shows. It matters. We can feel it, and the people who surround us feel it. We can enjoy it—literally, it brings us into joy. When we finally trust that we can love and be loved without being hurt, we are able to tap into our connection to others and to the world around us.

Staying clean for a long time means not just that recovery happens, but that life happens. We grow up and grow old; we raise families, change jobs, and navigate the world just because we are alive and clean. We come to understand that happiness is an inside job, a spiritual experience that can get stronger with recovery. We find that no matter what happens on the outside, joy can still live within us. A member shared: "I embraced my feelings and found comfort in them because I knew they were part of my remaking. I was alive. As much as it felt like I might come undone, I had faith that it wasn't the end. I knew that absolutely nothing in the world mattered except love. I have wasted too much time not loving."

Love is a form of intelligence. It's the intuition that brings us to the right words when there are no words, that tells us when to step forward and when to back away. We feel love when we speak truth. When we are in our Higher Power's will, we naturally carry a message, and the message we need finds us. When we clear away the defects that block the passage, we can be a clearer channel for the love that surrounds us. We tap into a love that is greater than ourselves, and find that we are able to do things we never thought possible. Brilliance comes through us.

There's a saying in recovery that as we keep going, the road narrows. That's partly true. Our willingness to make the same old mistakes diminishes, and we know better than to act on our impulses much of the time. But that's not the end of the story. It's as if we pass through a funnel: The way gets tighter and more uncomfortable as we begin to adapt to our new way of life—and then, without warning, it opens up and we are free. The road is no longer narrow; sometimes it seems like there's no road at all. We move to our own rhythm, finding a pace and a direction that is right for us. The trip is inward and it never stops. We keep learning and growing, finding ways to live and to use our experience to help others. No matter how long we have been clean, there is still more for us to learn and more for us to share. Our First Step placed us on a path to awareness, connection, and serenity. We received much more than simple abstinence. We have been given an endless supply of principles to guide us as we travel through our lives.

In Step Three, we make a decision to turn our will over to a power greater than ourselves, and in Step Eleven it is returned to us, transformed. The desperation we once felt at our predicament was the opening to a passion for caring, sharing, giving, and growing. Where once we lacked the power even to keep ourselves alive, now we take action in our own lives and in service to others, and we are amazed at the results. We live with dignity, integrity, and grace—and we know we can always get better.

The more progress we recognize in ourselves and our fellows, the more we know is possible. What first appeared to us as a way out now offers us a way in—into a life we hadn't imagined, into joy, into hope, into growth that never stops. We continue to get better. We continue to discover new ways to live, new freedom, and new paths to explore. We travel together as one in fellowship, and we pave the road as we walk it for all who may follow. No matter how far we have come, or how far we know we have to go, when we live clean, the journey continues.